KEY
EMPLOYMENT
LAW

Chris Turner

KEY
CASES

KEY
CASES

HODDER
EDUCATION
AN HACHETTE UK COMPANY

Orders: please contact Bookpoint Ltd, 130 Milton Park, Abingdon, Oxon OX14 4SB.
Telephone: (44) 01235 827720. Fax: (44) 01235 400454. Lines are open from 9 am to 5 pm,
Monday to Saturday, with a 24-hour message answering service. You can also order
through our website www.hoddereducation.co.uk.

If you have any comments to make about this, or any of our other titles, please send
them to educationenquiries@hodder.co.uk.

British Library Cataloguing in Publication Data
A catalogue record for this title is available from the British Library.

ISBN: 978 1 444 17233 1

First edition published 2012
Impression number   10 9 8 7 6 5 4 3 2 1
Year   2015 2014 2013 2012

Hachette UK's policy is to use papers that are natural, renewable and
recyclable products and made from wood grown in sustainable forests.
The logging and manufacturing processes are expected to conform to the
environmental regulations of the country of origin.

Typeset by Datapage India Pvt Ltd
Printed in Great Britain for Hodder Education, an Hachette UK Company,
338 Euston Road, London NW1 3BH.

Contents

Table of cases

Preface

The Key Cases series is designed to give a clear understanding of important cases. This is useful when studying a new topic and invaluable as a revision aid.

Each case is broken down into fact and law. In addition many cases are extended by the use of important extracts from the judgment or by comment or by highlighting problems. In some instances students are reminded that there is a link to other cases or material. If the link case is in another part of the same Key Cases book, the reference will be clearly shown. Some links will be to additional cases or materials that do not feature in the book.

To give a clear layout, symbols have been used at the start of each component of the case. The symbols are:

 Key Facts – These are the basic facts of the case.

 Key Law – This is the major principle of law in the case, the *ratio decidendi*.

 Key Judgment – This is an extract from a judgement made on the case.

 Key Comment – Comments made on the case.

 Key Problem – Apparent inconsistencies or difficulties in the law.

 Key Link – This indicates other cases which should be considered with this case.

The Key Link symbol alerts readers to links within the book and also to cases and other material especially statutory provisions which are not included.

At the start of each chapter there are mind maps highlighting the main cases and points of law. In addition, within most chapters, one or two of the most important cases are boxed to identify them and stress their importance.

Each Key Cases book can be used in conjunction with the Key Facts book on the same subject. Equally they can be used as additional material to support any other textbook.

This Key Cases book on Employment Law starts with the influence of EU law, then considers employee status which is vital for employment protection of any kind, the contract, implied terms, some statutory protections including on wages, protection from discrimination now under the umbrella of the Equality Act 2010, health and safety, TUPE, and finally the law relating to termination of the contract of employment.

The law is as I believe it to be on 1st January 2012.

Chris Turner

1

The Importance of EU Membership to Employment Law

The importance of EU membership

Costa v ENEL 6/64 (1964)
Where applicable EU law takes precedent over inconsistent national law

Van Gend en Loos v Nederlandse Administratie der Belastingen 26/62 (1963)
Measures can be enforced if clear, precise and unconditional, and conferred rights

Von Colson and Kamann v Land Nordrhein-Westfalen (1984)
Since Member States have an obligation under Art 10 (now Art 4(3) TEU) to give full effect to EU law then they should interpret an improperly implemented directive so as to give effect to its objectives

Brasserie du Pecheur SA v Federal Republic of Germany; R v Secretary of State for Transport, ex p Factortame Ltd (1996)
Can sue state for failure to implement directives if clearly gives right, breach is sufficiently serious, and the citizen suffers loss caused by the breach of EU law

 ECJ   Costa v ENEL 6/64 [1964] ECR 585

Key Facts
Costa owned shares in a pre-privatised Italian electric company and argued that the law privatising the industry breached EU (then EC) competition law. Following a judgment in the Italian constitutional court, the Italian government argued that these proceedings were unlawful as the court should have followed the Italian law which came after that ratifying the Treaty.

Key Law

EU (then EC) law took precedence over inconsistent national law even if it was introduced after the signing of the Treaty.

Key Judgment

The court stated: '*By contrast with ordinary international treaties, the EC Treaty [now the Treaty on the Functioning of the European Union, or TFEU] has created its own legal system which on entry into force ... became an integral part of the legal systems of the Member States and which their courts are bound to apply ... the Member States have limited their sovereign rights ... and have thus created a body of law which binds both their nationals and themselves ... The transfer, by Member States from their national orders in favour of the Community [now EU] order of its rights and obligations arising from the Treaty, carries with it a clear limitation of their sovereign right upon which a subsequent unilateral law, incompatible with the aims of the Community cannot prevail. ... It follows ... that the law stemming from the Treaty ... could not, because of its special and original nature, be overridden by domestic legal provisions, however framed, without being deprived of its character as Community law and without the legal basis of the Community itself being called into question.*'

Key Comment

This is the first clear definition and explanation of the consequences of the doctrine of supremacy of EU law.

Key Links

Van Gend en Loos v Nederlandse Administratie der Belastingen 26/62 [1963] ECR 1, [1963] CMLR 105 which gave the very first statement on supremacy.

International Handelsgesellschaft GmbH v EVGF 11/70 [1970] ECR 1125, [1972] CMLR 255 which extended the principle to include national constitutional principles.

Simmenthal SpA v Amministrazione delle Finanze dello Stato 70/77 [1978] ECR 1453, [1978] 3 CMLR 670 which identified that supremacy applies whether the national rule comes before or after the EC (now EU) rule.

R v Secretary of State for Transport ex p Factortame Ltd C-213/89 [1990] ECR I-2433

Key Facts

Certain UK registered companies involved in trawling were mostly owned by Spanish nationals. The Merchant Shipping Act 1988 and the Merchant Shipping (Registration of Fishing Vessels) Regulations 1988 required that a certain percentage of ownership should be in the hands of UK nationals. In the English court the applicants argued that the requirement was in breach of Art 18 (then Art 6) as it discriminated on nationality, as a result of which they were denied fishing rights otherwise guaranteed by EU (then EC) law.

Key Law

The problem for the House of Lords (now the Supreme Court) was whether to grant an interim injunction against an Act of Parliament, enacted after membership which specifically contradicted EC (now EU) law. The effect would be to suspend operation of the Act until the issue could be settled in a reference to the ECJ. The court recognised that there was no rule in English constitutional law that would allow the injunction. In its reference the question was whether, in order to protect EC (now EU) rights, a national court must grant the interim suspension of an Act of Parliament. The ECJ held, to give effect to EC (now EU) law, it must.

Key Judgment

The ECJ stated: '*It is for the national courts in application of the principle of co-operation ... to set aside national legislative provisions which might prevent, even temporarily, [EU] rules from having full force and effect ... It therefore follows that a court which in those circumstances would grant interim relief, if it were not for a rule of national law, is obliged to set aside that law.*'

Key Comment

The case represents the most far-reaching statement of supremacy of EU law over national law and the concept of supranationalism.

Key Links

Macarthys Ltd v Smith [1979] 1 WLR 1189. It also contrasts with the earlier views expressed by Lord Denning: 'If the time should ever come when our Parliament deliberately passes an Act with the intention of repudiating the Treaty or any provisions in it, or intentionally of acting inconsistently with it, and says so in express terms, then I should have thought that it would be the duty of our courts to follow the statute of our Parliament.'

(ECJ) **Van Gend en Loos v Nederlandse Administratie der Belastingen 26/62 [1963] ECR 1**

Key Facts

The Dutch government increased import duty on a chemical imported from Germany causing increased cost to a Dutch bulb grower. He argued that this breached Art 30 (then Art 12). The Dutch government argued that a citizen could not invoke rights granted under the Treaties. In the reference the question was whether a Treaty Article could create rights which nationals could enforce in national courts.

Key Law

The Advocate-General's reasoned decision suggested that, since the Article contained no explicit mention of individual rights, it could not be construed as granting individual rights and that the appropriate action should be under Art 258 (then Art 169) proceedings. The ECJ held that, since the Treaty was clearly intended to affect individuals, although the Article did not mention rights, it must clearly be capable of creating rights enforceable by individuals in national courts.

Key Judgment

The ECJ stated: *'Independently of the legislation of the Member States Community [now EU] law … not only imposes obligations on individuals but is also intended to confer upon them rights which become part of their legal heritage … not only where they are expressly granted by the Treaty, but also by reason of obligations which the Treaty imposes in a clearly defined way upon individuals … Member States and the institutions of the Community [now EU].'* It added *'The fact that the Article enables the Commission and the Member States to bring before the court a State which has not fulfilled its obligations does not mean that individuals cannot plead these obligations. [Such] a restriction … would remove all direct legal protection of the individual rights of their nationals.'*

Key Comment

The ECJ thus developed the principle of direct effect in the case which is simply the ability of an EU citizen to enforce rights granted under the Treaties.

Von Colson and Kamann v Land Nordrhein-Westfalen 14/83 [1984] ECR 1891

Key Facts

Joined Art 267 (then Art 177) references involved the improper implementation of directive 76/207 (now in the Recast Directive 2006/54) by the German government in the failure to provide adequate compensation under national law by contrast to full compensation required by the directive. Von Colson had applied to work for a state body, the prison service, while Harz had applied to work for a private company. Both were discriminated against contrary to the Directive.

Key Law

The ECJ held that the failure of German law to provide the proper levels of compensation was incomplete implementation of the Directive. However, while Von Colson could have

gained a remedy through vertical direct effect because the
employer in question was the state, Harz would have been
denied a remedy because of the anomaly resulting from lack
of horizontal effect. The ECJ took a novel approach in resolv-
ing this problem. It employed the obligation in Art 5 EC
Treaty (now Art 4(3) Treaty on European Union (TEU)) requiring Member States to give full effect to EU (then EC) law and
introduced the principle of 'indirect effect'. The German court
was bound to give full effect to the Directive so had to order
full compensation in both cases.

Key Judgment

The court stated: *'Since the duty under [Art 5] to ensure fulfil-
ment of [an] obligation was binding on all national courts ... it
follows that ... courts are required to interpret their national law in
the light of the wording and purpose of the Directive'.*

Key Problem

The ECJ ignored the problems created by the absence of
horizontal direct effect of Directives. It created instead a
means of overcoming those problems. Nevertheless, the
judgment did leave ambiguous the question of to which
national law the process of indirect effect could actually
apply. This then allowed the House of Lords to refuse to
apply the principle in *Duke* even though it would have been a
means of providing a remedy for the applicant.

Key Link

The same failure was seen in the second *Marshall* case, *Marshall
v Southampton and South West Hampshire AHA (No 2) C-271/91.*

Marleasing SA v Commercial Internacional de Alimentacion SA C-106/89 [1990] ECR I-4135, [1992] 1 CMLR 305

Key Facts

A company argued that another company was void under
the Spanish Civil Code. That other company sought to rely on
Directive 68/151 (on company law harmonisation). This listed
all the grounds for invalidating companies but did not include

that particular ground. Spain had not implemented the Directive at all, in contrast to the incomplete implementation in *Von Colson*.

Key Law

In a reference to the ECJ, the question was whether the applicant could rely on the rules on the constitution of companies in Directive 68/151 since this conflicted with Spanish law. The ECJ applied the principles of indirect effect and held that the Spanish court was bound to give effect to the Directive.

Key Judgment

The ECJ explained: *'In applying national law, whether the provisions concerned pre-date or post-date the Directive, the national court asked to interpret national law is bound to do so in every way possible in the light of the text and the aims of the directive to achieve the results envisaged by it.'*

Key Comment

The case increased the scope of indirect effect significantly, and has the effect of introducing horizontal direct effect by an indirect means, hence the title given to the process.

Francovich v Italian Republic C-6 and C-9/90 [1991] ECR I-5357

Key Facts

Italy failed to introduce a scheme required by Directive 80/987 to provide set minimum compensation for workers on insolvency of their employers. As a result of the failure to properly implement the Directive the claimants who had been made unemployed could not recover compensation due to them.

Key Law

The ECJ held that Italy was in breach of its obligations and, since the claimants had no other remedy, the state was liable to compensate them for the loss resulting from its failure to implement the Directive. The court introduced the principle that citizens can sue the state for non-implementation of a Directive. It also confirmed that liability was not unlimited so that three conditions must be met:

- the Directive must confer rights on individuals
- the contents of those rights must be identifiable in the wording of the measure
- there must be a causal link between the damage suffered and the failure to implement the Directive.

Key Judgment

The ECJ stated: '*The full effectiveness of Community [now EU] rules would be impaired and the rights they recognise would be undermined if individuals were unable to recover damages where their rights were infringed by a breach of EC [now EU] law attributable to a Member State.*'

Key Problem

The ECJ left a number of questions unanswered and left the issue of determining the extent of liability to the national courts.

Brasserie du Pecheur SA v Federal Republic of Germany; R v Secretary of State for Transport, ex p Factortame Ltd (No 2) C-46 and 48/93 [1996] ECR I-1029

Key Facts

In joined references a German beer purity law was challenged on the basis that it that was in breach of Art 34 (then Art 28) TFEU, which prohibits quantitative restrictions on imports or exports or measures having an equivalent effect, and quotas under the Merchant Shipping Act 1988 were challenged as breaching Art 49 (then Art 52) on rights of establishment. The reference was to clarify the conditions for state liability.

Key Law

The court redefined the conditions from *Francovich* to:

- the rule of Community law infringed must be intended to confer rights on individuals;
- the breach must be sufficiently serious to justify liability;
- there must be a direct causal link between the breach of the obligation imposed on the state and the damage actually suffered by the applicant.

Key Comment

The case widens the definition of the state to include acts and omissions of any organ of the state. The scope of liability is also extended beyond Directives to include any breach of Community law, regardless of whether or not it has direct effect.

2

Employment Status

Testing employment status

Performing Rights Society Ltd v Mitchell and Booker (1924)
The control test depends on the nature and degree of detailed control over the person alleged to be an employee

Stevenson, Jordan & Harrison v MacDonald & Evans (1952)
A contract of service involves work being done as an integral part of the business but a contract for services means work, while done for the business, is not integrated into it but only accessory to it

Ready Mixed Concrete (South East) Ltd v Minister of Pensions and National Insurance (1968)
Three considerations for employment: payment of wages in return for work; agreement to submit to the control of the other; nothing inconsistent with a contract of employment

Carmichael v National Power plc (1999)
Employment involves mutuality of obligations, the employer is bound to provide work and the employee is bound to do it

 KB Performing Rights Society Ltd v Mitchell and Booker [1924] 1 KB 762

 Key Facts
A band of musicians, under its contract, was bound not to play anything that was subject to copyright, but did so. The claimant sued the company hiring the musicians.

 Key Law
The court held that the musicians acted within the scope of their employment so the company was liable for the breach of copyright.

 Key Judgment
McCardie J stated: *'The test … lies in the nature and degree of detailed control over the person alleged to be the servant.'*

Mersey Docks & Harbour Board v Coggins & Griffith [1947] AC 1

 Key Facts

The Board hired out a crane to stevedores and a driver to operate it. Under the contract between the Board and the stevedores the Board were to pay the driver and only it had the right to dismiss him, but during the contract he was employed by the stevedores. The crane driver negligently injured a person in the course of his work and the issue was who was liable.

 Key Law

It was held that the Board was the employer at the material time since it was in control of him and it could not show that liability for his negligence had shifted to the stevedores. Although it could tell him what work to do it could not tell him how to operate the crane.

 Key Judgment

Lord Porter explained how the control test works *'to ascertain who is the employer at any particular time ... ask who is entitled to tell the employee the way in which he is to do the work upon which he is engaged... it is not enough that the task to be performed should be under his control, he must control the method of performing it'.*

Stevenson, Jordan & Harrison v MacDonald & Evans [1952] 1 TLR 101

 Key Facts

An accountant sold the copyright of a book produced partly through information gained generally during his employment and partly through a particular assignment that he had been given without which he would have had no such knowledge. The employer sought to restrain the transfer of copyright.

 Key Law

It was held that the employer could only restrain those parts of the manuscript relating to the specific knowledge gained during employment, not general knowledge.

Key Judgment

Lord Denning explained: '... *under a contract of service a man is employed as part of the business and his work is done as an integral part of the business but under a contract of services his work, although done for the business, is not integrated into it but only accessory to it*'.

(QBD) Market Investigations v Minster of Social Security [1969] 2 QB 173

Key Facts

Interviewers employed on a casual basis by a market research company needed to prove that they were employees in order that the company should pay their National Insurance contributions. The interviewers were obliged to complete their surveys within an allotted time and were given set questions to ask. However, they were able to select their own times of working.

Key Law

Weighing up all factors in the case, the interviewers were held to be employees rather than independent contractors. Control was one element but did not wholly determine employment status.

Key Judgment

Cooke LJ commented that: '*No exhaustive list has been compiled and perhaps no exhaustive list can be compiled of considerations which are relevant in determining [employment status] ... control will no doubt always have to be considered, although it can no longer be regarded as the sole determining factor; and that factors, which may be of importance, are ... whether the man performing the services provides his own equipment, whether he hires his own helpers, what degree of financial risk he takes, what degree of responsibility for investment and management he has, and whether and how far he has an opportunity of profiting from sound management in the performance of his task.*'

(QBD) Ready Mixed Concrete (South East) Ltd v Minister of Pensions and National Insurance [1968] 2 QB 497

Key Facts

Under a new contract drivers were obliged to use vehicles, which they bought on hire purchase agreements from the company, in the company colours and logo. Vehicles also had to be maintained according to set standards and drivers could only use them on company business. Hours were flexible and pay was subject to an annual minimum rate based on concrete hauled. The contract also permitted them to hire drivers in their place. The question was who paid National Insurance contributions, the company or the drivers.

Key Law

It was held that the terms of the contract were inconsistent with a contract of employment and that the driver was self-employed.

Key Judgment

McKenna J developed the economic reality test: '(i) The *servant agrees that in consideration of a wage or other remuneration he will provide his own work and skill in the performance of some services ...; (ii) he agrees, expressly or impliedly, that in the performance of that service he will be in the other's control in a sufficient degree to make that other master; (iii) the other provisions of the contract are consistent with it being a contract of service.'*

Key Comment

The case developed the economic reality test, sometimes known as the multiple test, since all the various factors need to be considered.

 (CA) **Massey v Crown Life Insurance [1978] ICR 590**

Key Facts

A branch manager of an insurance company asked to change his employment relationship so that he could be paid his gross wages and make his own tax and National Insurance contributions. This would benefit him as he could pay annually on a previous year basis and claim expenses against tax. He formed himself into a business and did other work besides through it. The company later terminated his contract and he claimed unfair dismissal. In order to do so he had to show that he was an employee.

Key Law

The court held that, while there was no intention to defraud the revenue, the new agreement between the claimant and the company was a genuine attempt to change his status from employed to self-employed for all the benefits that this would bring. He could not therefore fall within unfair dismissal legislation.

(CA) O'Kelly v Trust House Forte [1984] QB 90

Key Facts

The company employed only 34 permanent staff but 200–300 casual staff. The claimants were on a list of around 100 who were given preference when work was available. They claimed that they had been unfairly dismissed for taking part in trade union activities.

Key Law

The claimants had no action since, as casual workers, they were subject to individual contracts for services and were therefore not employees and not eligible under unfair dismissal law.

Key Judgment

Sir John Donaldson MR identified that: *'Giving the claimants' evidence its fullest possible weight, all that could emerge was an umbrella or master contract for, not of, employment. It would be a contract to offer and accept individual contracts of employment and, as such, outside the scope of the unfair dismissal provisions.'*

(HL) Carmichael v National Power plc [1999] ICR 1226

Key Facts

The claimants worked on a 'casual' as required basis for the Central Electricity Generating Board (CEGB) as guides at a power station as stated in documents inviting applications for the posts. They had worked for CEGB for more than six years and had latterly done as much as 25 hours per week. The Court of Appeal stated that this meant the employer had an obligation to offer them a reasonable amount of work and they had a corresponding obligation to accept a reasonable amount of work, i.e. they had a contract of employment.

Key Law

The House of Lords (now the Supreme Court) reinstated the view adopted by the tribunal that, as casual workers, they were not in any contractual relationship with CEGB when they were not acting as guides, and therefore they were not employees.

Key Judgment

Lord Irvine LC identified that: *'The documents did no more than provide a framework for a series of* ad hoc *contracts of service or for services which the parties might subsequently make ... The parties incurred no obligations to provide or accept work but at best assumed moral obligations of loyalty in a context where both recognised that the best interests of each lay in being accommodating to the other ... their case founders on the rock of absence of mutuality.'*

Nethermere (St Neots) v Taverna and Gardiner [1984] IRLR 240

Key Facts

Outworkers (from home) in the garment industry had no fixed hours but used machines provided for them. The only rule was that they must do sufficient work to make it worthwhile for the company driver to collect. They needed to prove that they were employees.

Key Law

It was held that the longstanding relationship meant that there was mutuality of obligations. The company was bound to provide work and they were bound to do it.

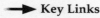

Key Links

Airfix Footwear Ltd v Cope [1978] IRLR 396 EAT

CA Cassidy v Minister of Health [1951] 2 KB 323

Key Facts

A resident surgeon performed an operation negligently and the patient sued. The issue for the court was whether the surgeon could be said legitimately to be under the employer's control because if not this would limit the patient's ability to receive compensation.

Key Law

It was held that hospitals must inevitably be vicariously responsible for the tortious acts of all doctors who are permanent members of staff despite the difficulties associated with applying the traditional control test, since to do otherwise would generally be to deny wronged patients an effective claim.

Key Judgment

Lord Somervell saw the difficulty by contrasting with the master of a ship: *'The master may be employed by the owners in what is clearly a contract of service and yet the owners have no power to tell him how to navigate his ship.'* Lord Denning stated: *'Authorities who run a hospital, be they local authorities, government boards, or any other corporation, are in law under the self-same duty as the humblest doctor. Whenever they accept a patient for treatment, they must use reasonable care and skill to cure him of his ailment.'*

CA Dacas v Brook Street Bureau [2004] ICR 1437

Key Facts

The claimant had been supplied by the agency and had worked for a local council as a cleaner for over four years when the council asked the agency to remove her. When the agency terminated its agreement with her she claimed unfair dismissal against both the council and the agency.

Key Law

The tribunal found that she was not an employee of either body. The EAT held that she was an employee of the agency. In the agency's appeal the Court of Appeal held that there was an implied contract with the council because of mutuality of obligations and length of service.

➤ **Key Links**

Montgomery v Johnson Underwood Ltd [2001] IRLR 269 where CA held an agency worker is not employed by the agency.

3

The Contract of Employment

Formation

Wishart v National Association of CAB'x Ltd (1990)
A contract can be subject to conditions precedent

De Francesco v Barnum (1890)
A minor is only bound by a contract that is substantially to his benefit

Coral Leisure Group Ltd v Barnett (1981)
Illegality only makes the whole contract void if it was entered into for an illegal purpose

The s 1 statement

System Floors v Daniel (1981)
The s 1 statement is evidence of the contract but only contractual if signed as such

Incorporation of express terms

Nelson v BBC (No 2) (1980)
Express written terms usually take precedence e.g. over oral undertakings after the contract is formed

Works rules

Secretary of State for Employment v Associated Society of Locomotive Engineers and Firemen (No 2) (1972)
Rules must not be followed in such a way as would damage the employer

Restraint of trade

Herbert Morris Ltd v Saxelby (1916)
Restraint clauses can only protect the employer's legitimate business interests and must be reasonable

Home Counties Dairies Ltd v Skilton (1970)
In geographical extent and duration they must not be too wide

The contract of employment

Collective agreements

Henry v London General Transport Services Ltd (2002)
If incorporated into the contract are generally binding

Garden leave

William Hill Organisation Ltd v Tucker (1999)
A decision to not provide work must be reasonable

Grievance procedure

W A Goold (Pearmak) Ltd v McConnell (1995)
Failure to provide a proper grievance procedure is a breach of contract

Disciplinary procedure

Brooks & Son v Skinner (1984)
Disciplinary rules are only binding if brought to the employee's attention

3.1 Formation of the contract of employment

CA Wishart v National Association of CAB'x Ltd [1990] IRLR 393

Key Facts

The claimant had been offered a position subject to satisfactory references. One of the references was from his existing employer which included information about several sickness absences. The employer who offered the claimant the job then withdrew the offer. The claimant sought an injunction to restrain that employer from taking on anyone else and enforcing his original job offer.

Key Law

Initially the injunction was granted. However, on appeal this was reversed. The Court of Appeal held that the job offer had been given subject to a condition, the receipt of satisfactory references. The employer's only obligation then was to consider the reference in good faith.

Ch De Francesco v Barnum (1890) 45 ChD 430

Key Facts

A 14-year-old entered a seven-year dancing apprenticeship with De Francesco. Under the apprenticeship deed she was bound to be at his total disposal, to accept no professional work without his express approval, and she was not allowed to marry without his permission. He was under no obligation to maintain her or to provide employment, but if he did the pay was very low. He was also able to terminate the arrangement without notice. When she accepted other work De Francesco sought to prevent it and failed.

Key Law

The apprenticeship deed was held to be unfair and unenforceable against her since it was not substantially for her benefit.

(EAT) Coral Leisure Group Ltd v Barnett [1981] IRLR 204

Key Facts

 The employee was a public relations executive. Among his duties he allegedly kept rich gamblers by providing the services of prostitutes for them. When he was later dismissed the issue was whether or not the contract was tainted with illegality meaning that he would have no claim in unfair dismissal.

Key Law

 It was held that an immoral or illegal act would not necessarily make the whole contract illegal unless the contract was entered into with the specific purpose of carrying out the illegal acts.

3.2 The s 1 statement

(CA) Robertson v British Gas [1983] ICR 351

Key Facts

 In his letter of appointment a gas meter reader was promised that he was included in an incentive bonus scheme which had been negotiated with the trade union. The employer later withdrew the bonus scheme and this was inserted in the s 1 statement, which the employee did not actually receive for seven years. The employee claimed for full arrears of the bonus.

Key Law

 The court held that the letter of appointment claimed a binding contractual term in relation to the bonus. Despite the collective agreement between the employer and the union having no legal force as between the signatories it was incorporated into the employee's contractual terms. The withdrawal of the bonus scheme was thus a unilateral change to the contract.

Key Problem

The case shows that unless signed as a contract of employment the s 1 statement is only evidence of contractual terms. Other evidence includes the letter of appointment. So it is important to look at all evidence to establish what the terms of the contract actually are.

System Floors v Daniel [1981] IRLR 475

 Key Facts

The claimants had signed a document which it was accepted was mere acknowledgement of receipt of the statutory statement provided by the employer. The claimants wished to claim unfair dismissal so needed to establish the precise date of their employment. The date was disputed by the parties and the precise status of the s 1 statement needed to be established by the court.

 Key Law

The court held that the s 1 statement is not definitive of the contractual terms unless the parties stipulate that it is. It is very strong but not conclusive evidence of terms in the contract. However, it does place a heavy burden on the employer to show how and why the terms of the contract differ from those identified in the statement.

 Key Judgment

Browne-Wilkinson P stated: *'The statutory statement ... provides very strong* prima facie *evidence of what were the terms of the contract between the parties, but does not constitute a written contract between the parties.'*

CA Gascol Conversions Ltd v Mercer [1974] IRLR 155

 Key Facts

Under a national agreement (with the trade union) employees worked 40 hours a week, plus overtime if necessary. Under a local agreement (within the company) the working week was 54 hours. When the claimant was made redundant the issue was on which of these should his redundancy payment be calculated.

 Key Law

The court held that the national agreement was incorporated into his contract and took precedence over the local agreement because it was actually reflected in the s 1 statement.

3.3 The incorporation of express terms

CA Nelson v BBC (No 2) [1980] IRLR 346

Key Facts

Under his contract an employee was required to work when and where the corporation demanded. When the employer closed down its Caribbean service it tried to make him redundant on the basis that it was implied in the contract that he was only required for that service.

Key Law

The court held that there was no such implied term. The express term in the contract on place of work was absolutely clear and unambiguous. Therefore there could be no redundancy.

CA Judge v Crown Leisure Ltd [2005] EWCA Civ 571

Key Facts

The employee attended a staff Christmas party during which he was promised to be put on 'roughly' the same pay scale as other managers. When he was not he claimed breach of contract.

Key Law

It was held that the words used were too vague to be contractually binding. This is merely a reflection of the rule that an offer must be certain as to its terms.

EAT United Bank Ltd v Akhtar [1989] IRLR 503

Key Facts

An employee's contract included a mobility clause. The employer notified the employee that he was to transfer from the Birmingham branch to the Leeds branch about 120 miles away. He was given only three days' notice and, despite his pleas for a brief delay in his transfer because of his wife's serious illness at the time and in order to sort out arrangements, the employer refused. He left claiming constructive dismissal.

Key Law

The court held that, even though there was a mobility clause in the contract, there was an implied term that it should be affected in a reasonable manner. As a result there was a successful claim of unfair dismissal.

3.4 Collective agreements

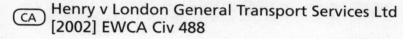

Henry v London General Transport Services Ltd [2002] EWCA Civ 488

Key Facts

A business was being sold to management. In preparation for the transfer the employer held negotiations with a trade union in which various changes to the contract, including a reduction in pay, were agreed. Following meetings with its members the union then informed the management that the majority of staff had consented to the changes which were then put into effect. Two employees objected to the new pay scales and brought an action for unlawful deductions from their wages.

Key Law

The court held that because of the history of collective agreements in the business it meant that the changes made in the collective agreement were incorporated into the contract and were binding.

Alexander v Standard Telephones and Cables plc [1990] IRLR 55

Key Facts

A collective agreement between management and a trade union identified that any compulsory redundancies would be based on a last in first out (LIFO) criterion. The company, in a redundancy situation, wished to retain employees on the basis of their skills and flexibility. The claimant sought an injunction to prevent this.

Key Law

It was accepted that the agreement was incorporated into his contract so that any remedy could only be for breach of the contract, if indeed there was any breach in the circumstances.

3.5 Works rules

(EAT) Dryden v Greater Glasgow Health Board [1992] IRLR 469

Key Facts

The employer, after extensive consultation, introduced a no smoking policy within the workplace. The employee who usually smoked up to thirty cigarettes per day had been used to smoking while at work in areas that were set aside for that purpose. She decided that she could no longer remain at work under the prohibition and claimed constructive dismissal.

Key Law

The court held that there was no breach of contract since there was neither any implied term nor any customary term that she could smoke. The rule was for a legitimate purpose and it did not prevent the employee from performing her contract.

Key Comment

Interestingly legislation has subsequently meant that not only can smoking not take place in the workplace but in any proscribed public place.

Secretary of State for Employment v Associated **(CA)** Society of Locomotive Engineers and Firemen (No 2) [1972] 2 QB 455

Key Facts

During an industrial dispute over pay, railway workers engaged in a so-called 'work to rule'. This involved not working overtime, including rest days. The action was clearly designed to cause inconvenience to the employer that depended on such flexibility to run its services effectively. Under the then Industrial Relations Act 1971 the Secretary of State was empowered to bring action against trade unions in disputes that might cause harm to the national economy.

Key Law

One of the obvious problems for the court was that if the employees were genuinely sticking to the rule book and this was in fact part of their contract then they could only be said to be honouring their contractual obligations. However, the court made reference to another part of the rule book which required that employees should 'make every effort to facilitate the working of trains and prevent unavoidable delay'. As such the employees were required to interpret the rules reasonably and not in such a way that would disrupt services and they were thus in breach of contract. This was despite the fact that Lord Denning identified that the rules were not in fact terms of the contract.

(EAT) Jeffries v BP Tanker Co Ltd [1974] IRLR 260

Key Facts

A company rule identified that employees with a history of cardiac disease could not work as radio officers at sea. The claimant had two heart attacks and was dismissed.

Key Law

It was held to be a fair dismissal even though the employee had made a full recovery and the rule was in essence a company policy.

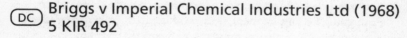

(DC) Briggs v Imperial Chemical Industries Ltd (1968) 5 KIR 492

Key Facts

A process worker at a cyanide plant was asked to move to another plant when management decided that the plant where he worked was to be demolished and replaced. He refused to move and claimed that he should be entitled to a redundancy payment.

Key Law

The court analysed his contract of employment. This stated that his rate of pay could be changed according to the job he was to do. Besides this the works rules acknowledged the right to transfer him to another job and also made reference to wage rates being variable according to whether the work was day work, night work, or shift work. As such the court concluded that these amounted to terms in his contract.

ⓘⓣ Singh v Lyons Maid Ltd [1975] IRLR 328

Key Facts

An employee who was a Sikh grew a beard which was in keeping with his religious beliefs. He did so despite knowing of a rule prohibiting the growing of beards. The rule was in place to maintain high standards of hygiene in a food-processing industry. His refusal to observe the rule led to his dismissal and he claimed unfair dismissal.

Key Law

The dismissal was held to be fair. In effect the employee had disobeyed a lawful and reasonable order which was necessary to the maintenance of proper conditions within the process.

3.6 Restraint of trade clauses

ⒽⓁ Herbert Morris Ltd v Saxelby [1916] 1 AC 688

Key Facts

A restraint clause in an employee's contract prevented him, after terminating his employment, from working in the sale or manufacture of pulley blocks, overhead runways, or overhead travelling cranes for a period of seven years after leaving. His employer's action failed.

Key Law

The court held that the restraint covered the whole range of the employer's business and the employee's potential expertise and was too wide to succeed despite the key position he had held and the experience he had gained from the employment. It would have deprived him of any employment opportunities.

ⒸⓗⒹ Forster v Suggett (1918) 35 TLR 87

Key Facts

A glass manufacturer included in the contracts of employees who were skilled glassblowers a clause that prevented them from working for any competitor on leaving their employment with him.

Key Law

The court held that the skill was so specialist at the time of the case that it amounted to a trade secret and the glass manufacturers were entitled to the protection of the clause. It was reasonable in the circumstances and was upheld.

CA Hanover Insurance Brokers Ltd and Christchurch Insurance Brokers Ltd v Schapiro [1994] IRLR 82

Key Facts

Christchurch bought brokerages which included Hanover Insurance Brokers (HIB). Three directors of HIB then left and formed their own brokerage. They were accused of soliciting clients contrary to a restraint clause in their contracts preventing them from soliciting the clients of Hanover Associates, which was a subsidiary of HIB. They argued that the clause was too wide and unreasonable and should be declared void as they had only ever worked for HIB.

Key Law

The court held that, since the purpose of the restraint was to prevent soliciting of insurance clients, and that only HIB engaged in this activity, the clause could be upheld against them.

Key Comment

The case also illustrates that the nature of the employee and his position within the business is also a determining factor.

HL Fitch v Dewes [1921] 2 AC 158

Key Facts

A restraint clause in the contract of a conveyancing clerk prevented him from taking up work of the same kind within a seven-mile radius of Tamworth Town Hall for an unlimited duration. The employee challenged the restraint.

Key Law

The restraint was still upheld as reasonable because of the rural nature of the community and the clerk's contact with the solicitor's client base. It did protect a legitimate business interest and it was reasonable.

(CA) Home Counties Dairies Ltd v Skilton [1970] 1 WLR 526

Key Facts

A milkman's contract contained two restraint clauses. Clause 12 prevented him from taking any employment connected with the dairy business. Clause 15 provided that he should not work as a milkman or serve any existing customer one year after leaving the employment.

Key Law

Clause 12 was held too wide to be reasonable. Potential areas of employment within the dairy industry were vast and the clause would have prevented him from taking a wide range of employment well beyond what he had done and with no chance of damaging his employer's interests. Clause 15 was enforced as it only protected legitimate interests and for only a short period.

(Ch) Eastham v Newcastle United FC Ltd [1964] Ch 413

Key Facts

George Eastham, a professional footballer, challenged the rules of the Football Association (FA) on the legitimacy of the transfer system as it then existed. Under the FA rules clubs could keep a player's registration even after his contract had ended and so effectively the rules could be used to prevent him from playing again. Besides this at the time players could be placed on the transfer list against their will. He claimed that this was an unlawful restraint of trade.

Key Law

The court determined that these rules did amount to an unlawful restraint of trade and were unenforceable. In essence they merely prevented employees from working and did not protect a legitimate proprietary interest.

➡ Key Links

Bosman v Royal Belgian Football Association and EUFA C- 415/93 [1995] ECR I-4921 has subsequently identified that such practices are contrary to Art 45 TFEU (Art 48 EC at the time) on free movement of workers where it involves inter-state transfers, and Art 101 TFEU (Art 85 EC at the time) on competition law.

3.7 Garden leave clauses

William Hill Organisation Ltd v Tucker
[1999] IRLR 313

Key Facts

A senior dealer for the organisation was required in his contract to give six months' notice but in fact gave only one as he wished to join a competitor. He was put on 'garden leave' and paid but told not to come to work. The employee refused to abide by the garden leave and the employer sought an injunction to restrain him from working for the competitor.

Key Law

It was held that the injunction failed on three grounds:

1. Firstly it was stated that an employee who holds a 'specific and unique post' is entitled to work to carry out his skills.
2. There was no express power in the contract permitting garden leave.
3. The courts would in any case view garden leave in the same light as restraint of trade which must be reasonable in its extent and used only to protect a legitimate business interest.

The terms of the contract pointed to this also since the employee was required to work the hours necessary to carry out his duties in a full and professional manner.

Key Judgment

Morritt LJ suggested: *'If the employer were to be entitled to keep his employee in idleness, the investment in its staff might be as illusory as the limited power of suspension would be unnecessary.'*

Key Links

SG & R Valuation Service v Boudrais [2008] IRLR 770 which qualified the position that those with a right to work in such circumstances hold it subject to a breach of contract indicating that they are not willing and ready to work.

(CA) Evening Standard Co Ltd v Henderson [1987] ICR 588

Key Facts

The contract of employment included twelve months' notice on either side. The employee also agreed not to work for a competitor (any rival newspaper). In fact he gave two months' notice and was proposing to join a rival newspaper for the remainder of his contractual notice period. His employer sought an injunction to restrain him from working for the competitor during that period.

Key Law

The court granted the injunction on the basis that the employer was prepared to pay him during the notice period and was also protecting a legitimate business interest and was acting reasonably in doing so.

(CA) Provident Financial Group plc v Hayward [1989] IRLR 84

Key Facts

The contract of a financial director of an estate agent included a clause that during his employment he would not work for anyone else. Although he was contractually obliged to give twelve months' notice, in agreement with his employer he actually gave six. He continued working for two months after which the employer decided that there was no more work for him and an agreement for paid garden leave was reached. One month later he announced his intention to work for another estate agent and his employer sought an injunction to prevent this during the notice period.

Key Law

The injunction was not granted. This was firstly because by this time there was only ten weeks of his six months' notice remaining but also because the evidence showed that taking up the new post could not cause damage to his old employer.

3.8 Grievance procedure

(EAT) W A Goold (Pearmak) Ltd v McConnell [1995] IRLR 516

Key Facts

Two sales representatives were employed on a salary and commission basis. When a new managing director was appointed after the company faced financial difficulties he introduced a new payment system and the men's pay dropped significantly. Despite their approaches their manager refused to do anything about it and the new managing director did likewise. They left claiming a constructive dismissal and brought a claim for unfair dismissal.

Key Law

The court held that the failure to provide any form of grievance procedure amounted to a fundamental breach of the contract. Their claim for unfair dismissal succeeded.

Key Judgment

Morison J explained: *'Parliament considered that good industrial relations requires employers to provide their employees with a method of dealing with grievances in a proper and [timely] manner ... the right to obtain redress against a grievance is fundamental.'*

(ET) Raspin v United News Shops Ltd [1999] IRLR 9

Key Facts

The employer, failing to follow agreed disciplinary procedures, dismissed the employee. The employee claimed unfair dismissal.

Key Law

The claim succeeded. The failure to follow the agreed procedure meant that the dismissal had no foundation.

3.9 Disciplinary procedure

(EAT) Brooks & Son v Skinner [1984] IRLR 379

Key Facts

The company had reached an agreement with the trade union representatives that employees who failed to return to work on the day after the work's Christmas party would be dismissed. Skinner failed to turn up and was dismissed. He claimed unfair dismissal on the basis that he had never been told about the decision to dismiss in such circumstances.

Key Law

His claim succeeded. It was held that he could not be subject to rules, particularly those leading to dismissal, without the rule having been brought to his attention or being given a proper hearing.

(CA) Jones v Lee and Guilding [1980] IRLR 67

Key Facts

A headmaster of a Catholic school was dismissed after he divorced and then remarried. Under his contract before he could be dismissed he was entitled to a hearing in front of the local education authority and to be represented at those proceedings. In the event the procedure was not followed and he sought an injunction.

Key Law

The court granted the injunction. The school could not dismiss without following the correct procedure.

(EAT) Fuller v Lloyds Bank plc [1991] IRLR 336

Key Facts

The employee had injured another person's face with a glass while in a public house on Christmas Eve. In disciplinary proceedings the employer took a number of statements from witnesses to the event but did not reveal these to the employee in keeping with its policy. After the employee was dismissed he claimed unfair dismissal arguing that the procedure was unfair.

Key Law

The tribunal held that the dismissal was not unfair since the employee knew the nature of the allegations against him. The EAT added that the procedure was not so flawed that it made the outcome unfair. So there was no general principle that the witness statements should be shown to the employee, only if the essence of the case against him was contained in the statements.

Kulkarni v Milton Keynes Hospitals NHS Trust [2009] EWCA Civ 789
(CA)

Key Facts

A doctor was accused of professional misconduct as it was alleged that he had engaged in an improper examination of a female patient and faced a disciplinary hearing.

Key Law

The court dealt with the issue of whether the doctor was entitled to legal representation. It stated *in obiter* that if the outcome of such proceedings was such that he may be prevented from working that Article 6 of the European Convention on Human Rights would require that he be allowed legal representation at the hearing.

R v Governors of X School [2010] EWCA Civ 1
(CA)

Key Facts

A school teacher was accused of inappropriate behaviour with a young person on work experience at the school and was taken through disciplinary procedure. If the complaint was established he might face not only dismissal but also being prohibited from working with young people and vulnerable adults. The issue was whether he was entitled to legal representation.

Key Law

The court held that, although the procedure was not the same as being subjected to criminal charges, the gravity of the allegations and the potential consequences if they were proven meant that he was entitled to legal representation.

4

Implied Terms

The process of implying terms

Sagar v Ridehalgh (1931)
Can be by custom if reasonable, certain and notorious

Mears v Safecar Security Ltd (1982)
Should consider all relevant circumstances and how the parties behaved during the contract

Implied terms

Implied duties of the employer

Herbert Clayton & Jack Waller Ltd v Oliver (1930)
There is no general right to work but there may be in piece work, commission-only work, and work that advances the employee's reputation

Malik v Bank of Credit and Commerce International (1997)
An employer is bound to respect mutual trust and confidence

Implied duties of the employee

Ottoman Bank v Chakarian (1930)
The employee is only bound to follow reasonable and lawful orders, not ones that place him in danger

Boston Deep Sea Fishing and Ice Co v Ansell (1888)
Employees are bound to give faithful service; making a secret profit from the employment breaches this duty

4.1 The process of implying terms

(CA) Sagar v Ridehalgh [1931] 1 Ch 310

Key Facts
A weaver sued his employer for deducting one shilling (now 5p) from his wages for work that was not up to standard.

Key Law
It was held that this was a customary practice in the Lancashire cotton mills and therefore was incorporated into the contract as an implied term because it was 'reasonable, certain and notorious'.

Key Judgment

Lawrence LJ stated: *'The [practice] is not unreasonable. The deductions are not arbitrary ... they are limited to the ... loss occasioned to the employer ... a trade [practice] allowing an employer to make deductions for bad work ... not exceeding a certain defined limit ... does not ... render [it] uncertain ... and it is reasonable that employers should not exact the full amount of the loss.'*

(CA) **Mears v Safecar Security Ltd [1982] IRLR 183**

Key Facts

An employee questioned the fact that he received no pay during sickness absence. There was in fact no reference to sick pay in the written terms.

Key Law

The court held that, before implying any term into a contract, the correct process was to consider all of the relevant circumstances including the way that the parties had behaved during the contract. It did consider that where there was insufficient information that the dispute should be settled in favour of the employee. However, it found that here there was evidence that there had been no intention to include such a term and that therefore this should have been included in the written terms.

Key Comment

The case pre-dates the Social Security Contributions and Benefits Act 1992 under which all employees would now be eligible for Statutory Sick Pay.

4.2 The implied duties of employers

(CA) Devonald v Rosser [1901] 2 KB 653

Key Facts

The claimant was a piece worker, in other words paid by the 'piece' of work rather than a set wage. When his employer ceased trading the employee was given one month's notice but no work to do. He sued for damages.

Key Law

It was held that there was an implied term in the case of piece workers that they be given enough work to make their normal earnings. As a result there was a breach of contract and he was awarded damages for the period equivalent to his normal earnings.

Collier v Sunday Referee Publishing Co [1940] 2 KB 647

(KB)

Key Facts

A newspaper sub-editor was kept on by new employers when the paper was sold to another group. However, he was not given any work to do, although he was paid, and claimed that this was a breach of an implied term.

Key Law

While recognising that there are specific circumstances in which an employer would be obliged to provide work, the court held that there was no overall obligation.

Key Judgment

Asquith J explained the position as follows: '*It is true that a contract of employment does not necessarily, or perhaps normally, oblige the master to provide the servant with work. Provided I pay my cook her wages regularly, she cannot complain if I choose to take any or all of my meals out.*'

Herbert Clayton & Jack Waller Ltd v Oliver [1930] AC 209

(HL)

Key Facts

Clayton was an actor who was given a lead role in a musical. He was later removed from the lead role and given a supporting role instead but refused to accept it. He sued for damages arguing that, because the employer had failed to provide him with proper work, this would damage his reputation and his chance to gain future employment.

Key Law

It was held that, in the circumstances, there was an implied duty on the part of the employer to provide him with appropriate work. He was awarded damages for the loss of opportunity resulting from his lowered reputation.

Key Comment

Ordinarily there will be no absolute 'right to work' and thus no obligation on an employer to provide an employee with work. However, as the court recognised there are limited circumstances where it is vital that the employee be given work. These would include piece work and commission-only work, but also situations like this where the employee is dependent on being allowed to perform in order to get further work.

Malik v Bank of Credit and Commerce International [1997] IRLR 462

Key Facts

The bank was accused of fraudulent dealing and went into liquidation. The claimant, a former employee of the bank, found it almost impossible to find new employment because of having worked for the bank and claimed that this had destroyed his own personal reputation. He appealed against an earlier decision not to award him compensation.

Key Law

The House of Lords (now the Supreme Court) held that the corrupt and fraudulent practices of the bank amounted to a breach of the implied duty of mutual trust and confidence.

CA Langston v AUEW [1974] ICR 180

Key Facts

Langston refused to join a trade union as was his right in law at the time. Fellow employees who were members of the union threatened strike action so, to avoid this, the employer suspended Langston on full pay for an indefinite period. Langston then sued the union for inducing a breach of contract arguing that he was being denied the right to work.

Key Law

The Court of Appeal agreed that in certain circumstances an employee does have the right to work in order to achieve job satisfaction and it does not matter that he is being paid full wages while being denied work.

Key Judgment

Lord Denning explained: '[A] man should be given the opportunity of doing his work when it is available and he is ready and willing to do it. A skilled man takes a pride in his work. He does not do it merely to earn money. He does it so as to make his contribution to the well-being of all. He does it so as to keep himself busy, and not idle. To use his skill, and to improve it. To have the satisfaction which comes of a task well done.'

Key Problem

Lord Denning's view conflicts with that expressed by the then National Industrial Relations Court when the case was remitted to it. It considered that there was no right to work regardless of anything to the contrary, for instance in the Universal Declaration of Human Rights, that these were merely policy considerations and did not interfere with the contract which was the determining factor.

Crossley v Faithful and Gould Holdings Ltd [2004] EWCA Civ 293

Key Facts

A senior employee asked to take early retirement because of ill health. His employer failed to inform him that this would adversely affect his entitlement under a permanent health insurance scheme. He claimed that the employer was in breach of an implied term to warn him about the effects of his retirement.

Key Law

The court held that there was no such term. As a senior employee he should have been aware of the implications and in any case had access to specialist advice. To imply a term that an employer was responsible for financial advice would be unreasonable.

Key Link

Scally v Southern Health and Social Services Board [1992] 1 AC 294 where the then House of Lords identified that an employer had a duty to take reasonable steps to bring benefits of schemes to the attention of employees who could not be reasonably expected to be aware of these themselves.

Spring v Guardian Assurance plc [1994] IRLR 460

 Key Facts

An employee of an insurance company was dismissed and was also prevented from gaining a position with another company because of a negligently prepared and highly unfavourable reference provided by the first employer. The employee claimed for damages in negligence.

 Key Law

The House of Lords (now the Supreme Court) held that the first employers were liable because of the reference and that employers are under a duty of care to their employers and so have a duty of care not to make negligent references. However the House was split on whether the *Hedley Byrne* principle on negligent misstatement should apply in the case.

 Key Comment

The case was a major breakthrough for employees finding themselves in the position of the claimant. Previously the only remedy would have been through proving defamation. Under defamation law they would have been prevented from seeing the reference unless they could prove malice. In negligence law they could do so through discovery of documents.

 Key Links

The rule on negligently prepared references has subsequently been developed in *Bartholomew v London Borough of Hackney* [1999] IRLR 246. The Court of Appeal identified that the duty was to ensure that only accurate information is provided and the impression created is not unfair. More recently in *Cox v Sun Alliance Life Ltd* [2001] IRLR 448 Lord Justice Mummery identified other key ingredients of the duty. The employer must believe in the truth of any information that he divulges and must also have reasonable grounds for that belief, and make a reasonably thorough investigation of the facts before providing the reference.

4.3 The implied duties of employees

(PC) **Ottoman Bank v Chakarian [1930] AC 277**

Key Facts

The employee was required to go to Constantinople (now Istanbul) where he had formerly been sentenced to death.

Key Law

It was held that he did not have to obey an order which might expose him to danger or to the risk of loss of liberty or life. Such an order was unreasonable.

(NIRC) **United Kingdom Atomic Energy Authority v Claydon [1974] ICR 128**

Key Facts

Under the written terms of the contract the employee was required to work anywhere in the United Kingdom. When he was asked to transfer to another site he refused and was dismissed as a result.

Key Law

It was held that the instruction was both lawful and reasonable because it was included in the express terms of the contract.

➤ **Key Link**

Bass Leisure Ltd v Thomas [1994] IRLR 104 (Chapter 9) where the EAT said that this principle on mobility clauses should not be followed. *High Table Ltd v Horst* [1998] ICR 409 which stated that the true test was a factual one and the existence of a mobility clause did not mean that an employee could automatically be transferred if his current place of work was his expected place of work. *United Bank Ltd v Akhtar* [1989] IRLR 503 which suggested that mobility clauses must be exercised reasonably.

(ChD) **Cresswell v Board of Inland Revenue [1984] 2 All ER 713**

Key Facts

The employee carried out clerical duties using paper filing systems. The employer then introduced a computerised system and the employee refused to accept training towards using those systems.

He argued that there was an implied term in his contract that he should not be required to carry out his work in a manner other than that which he had been used to, and claimed that the employer was therefore in breach of contract.

 Key Law

The court held that there was no such term but that there was an implied duty on the part of an employee to adapt to changing circumstances within the work environment which included adapting to new skills and methods as required for which an employer was bound to provide training.

(NIRC) Morrish v Henly's Ltd [1973] ICR 482

 Key Facts

An employee was asked by his employer to falsify some records. He refused and was later dismissed and claimed unfair dismissal.

 Key Law

It was held that the law only requires employees to obey reasonable and lawful orders. In this instance what the employee was asked to do was unlawful and thus any disciplinary action arising from it was unlawful also. The dismissal was unfair.

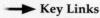 **Key Links**

Laws v London Chronicle [1959] 1 WLR 698.

(CA) Boston Deep Sea Fishing and Ice Co v Ansell (1888) 39 ChD 339

 Key Facts

The managing director of a company placed orders with another company from whom he was receiving a commission. When this was discovered he was dismissed and he challenged the decision.

 Key Law

The court held that the managing director's actions were a breach of the implied duty of faithful service or fidelity. One aspect of this duty is the duty not to make a secret profit, commission, gift or bribe from the employment because otherwise there is a conflict of interest. The dismissal was justified.

Key Comment

Of course the employee was also a director and therefore would have been under a fiduciary duty which he also breached.

(HL) Bell v Lever Bros [1932] AC 161

Key Facts

Lever Brothers employed Bell as chairman of an unsuccessful subsidiary company in order to improve its performance. This he successfully did so that the subsidiary was then merged with another company. Lever agreed a settlement of £30,000 for the termination of Bell's contract. It then discovered that Bell was in breach of a clause in his contract, prohibiting private dealings and sued unsuccessfully for return of the settlement.

Key Law

The House of Lords held that Bell was under no duty to reveal his own misconduct except in response to a direct question. Besides this there was no common mistake which would void the contract because the mistake was not operative. It was not the reason why Lever agreed the settlement. This was to reward Bell for the early termination of a completed contract which would have been part of its duty to pay for the work Bell had done.

Key Judgment

Lord Atkin said: *'In such a case, a mistake will not affect assent unless it is the mistake of both parties and is as to the existence of some quality which makes the thing without the quality essentially different from the thing as it was believed to be.'*

Key Problem

Lord Atkin accepted that a sufficiently fundamental mistake as to quality of the subject-matter can void a contract but refused to find this contract void. It has been argued that it is hard to imagine a more fundamental mistake and so the standard is set too high.

(CA) Sybron Corporation v Rochem Ltd [1983] ICR 801

Key Facts

The company made payments into the pension fund of its European Manager and when he retired he received a lump sum payment. The company then discovered that the manager had been conspiring with other colleagues to set up in direct competition with the company and it sought restitution of the lump sum payment. It argued that if it had known of the misconduct it could have dismissed the manager for gross misconduct representing a breach of the implied duty of fidelity.

Key Law

The court held that the money could be recovered since it was given under a mistake of fact and the breach of duty would have given rise to a right to dismiss the manager summarily.

Key Comment

This contrasts with *Bell v Lever Brothers* because here the mistake was the basis on which the contract was formed.

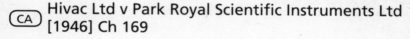

Hivac Ltd v Park Royal Scientific Instruments Ltd [1946] Ch 169

Key Facts

A skilled employee of a company involved in a technologically advanced business worked for a direct competitor in his spare time. The company sought an injunction to prevent this competition.

Key Law

The court held that the injunction could be granted in the circumstances. However it did point out that an injunction would not be possible where an employee merely worked part-time for a company operating a different type of business which was therefore not in competition. This would be to interfere with the employee's right to earn a living.

CA Faccenda Chicken v Fowler [1986] ICR 297

Key Facts

Fowler was sales manager of a company which sold fresh chickens. He developed a new sales strategy involving a door-to-door service. He then left to set up his own business in competition with his former company which sought an injunction to prevent this.

Key Law

The injunction was denied because there was no express restraint in the contract protecting the business interest.

5

Statutory Protections

Statutory protections

Maternity

***Webb v EMO Air Cargo (UK) Ltd* (1994)**
It is discriminatory to dismiss a woman because of her pregnancy

Parental leave and dependant care leave

***Qua v John Ford Morrison* (2003)**
Covers critical points where a child becomes ill, but not ongoing care

Wages

***Fairfield Ltd v Skinner* (1993)**
Deductions from pay can only be made if justified by fact

Guarantee payments

***Garvey v J & J Maybank (Oldham) Ltd* (1979)**
Not available if the lay-off occurs because of a trade dispute

5.1 Maternity

 Webb v EMO Air Cargo (UK) Ltd [1994] IRLR 482

Key Facts

A female worker was appointed by a small business with only sixteen employees to cover a maternity leave. When she was taken on, it was envisaged that she should be able to stay with the firm even after the end of the maternity leave that she was covering. After two weeks in employment she discovered that she was pregnant and was dismissed after informing her employer. She claimed unfair dismissal on the ground that the sole reason for her dismissal was her pregnancy and this was discrimination.

Key Law

The ECJ in the reference held that dismissing a female worker in an indefinite period of employment solely because of her pregnancy was unlawful discrimination contrary to Directive 76/207 (now in the Recast Directive 2006/54). The question left open by the court was whether the dismissal would be non-discriminatory and therefore lawful if the employment was for a definite period.

Key Link

Jiménez Melgar v Ayuntamiento de Los Barrios C-438/99 [2001] ECR I-6915 and *Teledenmark v Handels-og Kontorfuntionaerernes Forbund i Danmark* C-109/00 [2001] ECR I-6993. In both cases the ECJ held that no distinction should be drawn between pregnant workers on indefinite contracts and those on temporary contracts.

Dekker v Stichting Vormingscentrum voor Jonge Volwassen 177/88 [1991] IRLR 27

Key Facts

A pregnant woman was refused employment by a company because of her pregnancy and she argued that this was direct discrimination. The company argued that there were no male candidates for the post so there could be no discrimination when they had chosen from an exclusively female file of candidates.

Key Law

The ECJ rejected the company's argument and held that refusal to employ a woman on grounds of pregnancy was directly linked to her sex and was unjustifiable direct discrimination.

Key Judgment

The court identified that: *'A refusal of employment on account of the financial consequences of absence due to pregnancy must be regarded as based essentially on the fact of pregnancy [and] cannot be justified on grounds relating to the financial loss which an employer who appointed a pregnant woman would suffer for the duration of her maternity leave.'*

(ECJ) North Western Health Board v McKenna C-191/03 [2005] IRLR 895

Key Facts

The claimant was absent from work for most of her pregnancy and for some time after because of pregnancy-related illness. Her employer operated a scheme where employees were paid full pay for the first 183 days of sickness then half pay for the rest of any eighteen-month period. It also covered pregnancy-related illness prior to maternity leave. As a result the claimant spent some absence on half pay and argued that this was discrimination.

Key Law

The ECJ held that [EU] law did not require full pay during periods of pregnancy-related illness so long as pay rates during such periods did not defeat the objective of protecting pregnant workers.

(EAT) British Telecommunications plc v Roberts and Longstaffe [1996] IRLR 601

Key Facts

Two employees wished to return to work after maternity leave on a job-sharing arrangement. However, to do so they would be required to work on Saturday mornings. They complained that this was indirect discrimination.

Key Law

The court held that job-sharing did not come under the protections offered to women during pregnancy and maternity leave and therefore there was no issue of discrimination.

5.2 Parental leave and dependant care leave

(EAT) Qua v John Ford Morrison [2003] IRLR 184

Key Facts

A legal secretary had a number of absences from work during a short period. She claimed that this was justified under dependant care leave provisions as the absences were almost entirely to do with her son's medical problems.

Key Law

The EAT gave guidance on the application of dependant care leave. It held that such leave covered the immediate critical points where a child became ill and arrangements needed to be made, but did not include continuous ongoing care. In other words there is no right to unlimited time off for dependant care needs and a dismissal in such circumstances would not be classed as automatically unfair.

Key Links

Forster v Cartwright Black [2004] IRLR 781 where the EAT stated that leave on death of a dependant was for funeral arrangements and attending the funeral but not for overcoming grief.

(EAT) Atkins v Coyle Personnel plc [2008] IRLR 420

Key Facts

The claimant was on paternity leave during which he also worked and was available to answer phone calls. He was woken up to take one phone call from his manager having only had three hours' sleep. This led to a series of angry e-mails and an angry phone call after which he was dismissed. He claimed unfair dismissal.

Key Law

The tribunal identified that, for unfair dismissal purposes, the dismissal must be connected to the paternity leave. This was during the paternity leave but actually resulted from the angry exchanges and therefore was not connected to the paternity leave and was not therefore an automatically unfair dismissal.

(EAT) Blundell v St Andrew's Catholic Primary School [2007] IRLR 652

Key Facts

The claimant had taught the reception class in a primary school before she went on maternity leave. On her return, because of a policy of rotation of teachers every two years, she was asked to teach Year 2 and argued that she had not been properly returned to the job she was doing before she took her leave as required.

Key Law

The court held that she had in fact been returned to her job – that of primary school teacher. The exact teaching class was irrelevant to the protection offered.

5.3 Wages

Delaney v Staples t/a De Montfort Recruitment [1992] IRLR 191

Key Facts

The employee was summarily dismissed and given a cheque as payment in lieu of wages. The employer then stopped the cheque and justified this on the basis of the employee having taken confidential information with her. She then claimed that there had been an unlawful deduction from her wages. The issue then was whether the claim could be made in a tribunal or whether it had to be made in court.

Key Law

The House of Lords (now the Supreme Court) identified that payment in lieu of wages, where it relates to the period after employment, is not wages, which are for services rendered, but damages in anticipation of a breach of the contract by termination. Lord Browne-Wilkinson listed four circumstances where a lieu payment would be appropriate:

(i) the employer gives the appropriate notice but does not require work from the employee (garden leave)

(ii) under the contract the employer is entitled to terminate the contract with notice or summarily on payment of a sum of money in lieu of notice

(iii) an agreement between employer and employee to terminate the contract for an agreed payment

(iv) the employer dismisses the employee summarily with a lieu payment.

Key Comment

Since the Employment Tribunals Extension of Jurisdiction Order 1994 such actions can be heard in tribunals so the specific problem in the case has been removed.

(EAT) Fairfield Ltd v Skinner [1993] IRLR 4

Key Facts

A van driver was subject to a requirement that deductions would be made from his wages for private phone calls, private mileage and for excess insurance arising from damage to the van. After he was dismissed £305 was deducted from his final wage with half being for damage done to the van and the other half a notional fee for private phone calls. The employee claimed that this was an unlawful deduction under the Wages Act.

Key Law

The tribunal found that the employee had personally paid for damage to the van and that there was no evidence to show how deductions for phone calls were calculated so that the deductions were indeed unlawful. The EAT held that although an employer may have a right to make deductions, a deduction can only be made if it can be justified in fact. Since the employer's allegations were unsubstantiated there was no justification for the deduction.

(EAT) Kent Management Services Ltd v Butterfield [1992] IRLR 394

Key Facts

On termination of his contract an employee was arguing that *ex gratia* discretionary bonus payments should be counted as wages and therefore that he was entitled to them.

Key Law

The court held that such payments could indeed be classed as wages because it was in the contemplation of both parties that such payments would be made where appropriate under the scheme. The court also suggested *in obiter* that if such payments were only to be paid on satisfactory performance or for some other stipulation that this should be clearly expressed in the contract.

(EAT) Greg May (Carpet Fitters and Contractors) Ltd v Dring [1990] IRLR 19

Key Facts

The employee's contract stated that he would be entitled to accrued holiday pay on termination of his contract, but that this would not apply if he was dismissed for gross misconduct, as he in fact was. The employer did not pay his holiday pay and he argued that this was an unlawful deduction.

Key Law
The EAT confirmed that the arrangement was contractual and therefore was subject to his dismissal actually being for gross misconduct. Since the tribunal had found that it was not, the withholding of the holiday pay was an unlawful deduction.

5.4 Guarantee payments

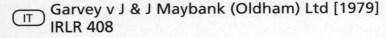

(IT) Garvey v J & J Maybank (Oldham) Ltd [1979] IRLR 408

Key Facts
The employee was a lorry driver who, along with other colleagues, had refused to cross a picket line during a dispute, in which he was not involved, between a trade union and his employer, despite the employer's instructions to the contrary. Because of the picket insufficient supplies were received by the employer to continue work and the employer then laid off workers, including the claimant, who argued that he was entitled to a guarantee payment by law.

Key Law
It was confirmed that guarantee payments during lay offs are not available if the workless day occurs because of a trade dispute involving any employee of the employer or associated employers. Since the lay off occurred because of the refusal of the drivers to cross the picket line, it was due to such a trade dispute and there was thus no entitlement to a guarantee payment.

6

Protection from Discrimination

Equal pay

Defrenne v SABENA (1976)
Art 119 (now 157 TFEU) directly effective

Cadman v Health and Safety Executive (2006)
Incremental pay scales can be justified if reflecting experience and capability

Hayward v Camell Laird Shipbuilders Ltd (No 2) (1988)
Can claim work of equal value

Sex

Johnston v Chief Constable of the Royal Ulster Constabulary (1987)
Only where gender is a determining factor is it an occupational requirement justifying discrimination

Bracebridge Engineering Ltd v Darby (1990)
Even a single unwanted offensive act is harassment and the employer is vicariously liable

Race

West Midlands Passenger Transport Executive v Singh (1988)
It is possible to introduce statistical data to show discrimination

Tottenham Green Under Fives' Centre v Marshall (1991)
Social and welfare needs may justify discrimination

Panesar v Nestle & Co (1980)
Dress code not discriminatory if needed for hygiene

Religion and belief

Azmi v Kirklees Metropolitan Borough Council (2007)
Dress code not discriminatory if dress not a doctrinal requirement

Discrimination

Age

Wolf v Stadt Frankfurt am Main (2010)
Capability linked to age can justify age limits

Disability

Chief Constable of Dumfries & Galloway v Adams (2009)
ME interferes with day-to-day activities so is an impairment

Farmiloe v Lane Group plc (2004)
Employer only bound to make reasonable adjustments not go to extraordinary lengths

Gender reassignment and sexual orientation

P v S and Cornwall CC (1996)
Transsexual discriminated against if treated less favourably than person of sex (s)he was before

English v Thomas Sanderson Blinds Ltd (2009)
Discrimination if harassed for being gay even if not gay

Trade unions

Bass Taverns Ltd v Burgess (1995)
Criticising employer in wrong context is not legitimate activity

Marley Tile Co Ltd v Shaw (1980)
Meetings in work time are not legitimate trade union activity

6.1 Equal pay

(ECJ) **Defrenne v SABENA 43/75 [1976] 2 CMLR 98**

Key Facts

Defrenne was employed as an air stewardess with the Belgian airline and was paid significantly less than male cabin crew. She was unable to claim equal pay under Belgian law as there was no legislation on equal pay. She tried to bring an action under Art 119 (now Art 157) and the Belgian authorities argued that the Article only affected the state and gave no rights to individuals.

Key Law

The court held that, since the Article complied with all of the *Van Gend en Loos* criteria for direct effect, in the absence of appropriate national law she could use the Article as the basis of her claim for equal pay. It also identified that the Article was both vertically and horizontally directly effective so could be used against private individuals as well as the state.

Key Judgment

The court stated that the prohibition on discrimination in pay *'applies not only to the actions of public authorities but also extends to all agreements which are intended to regulate paid labour collectively, as well as to contracts between individuals'*.

Key Problem

Unfortunately, following representations from the UK and Ireland, the Article was held to be only prospectively, not retrospectively, directly effective meaning that many women lost out on potential and justifiable claims in those countries.

(EAT) **Capper Pass Ltd v Lawton [1977] ICR 83**

Key Facts

A directors' cook was responsible for producing between 10 and 20 meals a day. She claimed equal pay with male chefs working in the works canteen. These produced around 350 meals per day in six sittings, two each for breakfast, lunch and tea. The men also had slightly different duties.

Key Law

Despite the differences in the work the woman was held to be working on like work and awarded equal pay.

Key Judgment

Phillips J explained: *'In most cases the inquiry will fall into two stages. First, is the work ... "of a broadly similar" nature ... secondly ... it is then necessary to go on to consider the detail and to enquire whether the differences between the work being compared are of "practical importance in relation to the terms and conditions of employment" ... There seems to be a tendency ... to weigh up the differences by references to such questions as whether one type of work is or is not suitable for women ... The only differences which will prevent work which is of a broadly similar nature from being "like work" are differences ... reflected in the terms and conditions of employment.'*

(EAT) Dugdale v Kraft Foods Ltd [1977] ICR 48

Key Facts

Four women were employed as quality control inspectors and claimed equal pay using six male quality control inspectors, who received a significantly higher basic rate of pay, as their comparators. The women worked only in mornings and afternoons. The men also worked in evenings, which were compulsory, and on Sunday mornings, which was voluntary, but for which they also received a 25% shift allowance. At the time women were prevented by law from working night shifts unless there was a specific statutory exemption (e.g. nurses) which did not apply here.

Key Law

The tribunal had held that the men and women did similar work but that the working at night was such a significant difference in working conditions that the men and women could not be said to be doing like work. The EAT concluded that the time at which the work is done is in itself no bar to equal pay but there is also no reason why the men should not be compensated for the more onerous hours through a shift allowance.

(EAT) Eaton Ltd v Nuttall [1977] ICR 272

Key Facts

A male and a female employee had broadly similar work but the man received greater pay because of certain responsibilities in that he worked with higher value products. The woman made a claim for equal pay using the man as her comparator.

Key Law

The court held that the difference in pay was justified, a genuine material factor, because his additional responsibilities meant that, for instance, if he made a mistake in his work it would be more costly to the employer and therefore the difference in the responsibilities was significant.

(ECJ) Rummler v Dato-Druck GmbH [1987] ICR 774

Key Facts

A female packer who was graded under her employer's job evaluation scheme below the level that she thought her work merited challenged the criteria used. These included muscular effort, physical hardship and fatigue.

Key Law

The ECJ held that the criteria used in job evaluation schemes must not differ according to whether the job is carried out by a man or by a woman. It also stated that it must not be organised in such a manner that it has the practical effect of discriminating against one sex. The criteria must be objectively justified and to be so they must be appropriate to the tasks to be undertaken and also correspond to a genuine need of the business. However, it also stressed that it would be possible to have criteria which included factors which favoured one sex over another provided that these criteria were part of an overall package which included factors that did not. In the scheme in question other criteria which were non-discriminatory included knowledge, training and responsibility.

Key Problem

Although the court focused on objective justification for particular criteria within an overall package that did not discriminate, in accepting physical strength as a criterion this would appear to naturally discriminate against women and in favour of men.

(HL) Pickstone v Freemans plc [1988] ICR 697

Key Facts

A female warehouse worker had both female and male colleagues who were all on the same pay. She made a claim for equal pay for work of equal value using a male checker who was on a higher rate of pay. The employer's argument was that there was no discrimination since there were both men and women being paid the same rate in the claimant's job.

Key Law

The court held that the fact that there was a man on the same rate of pay as the woman was irrelevant if there was a genuine need for equal pay with another male comparator. The House of Lords (now the Supreme Court) acknowledged that the alternative would be that unscrupulous employers would always be able to avoid equality by placing a token male on the same low pay as a woman.

(ECJ) Allonby v Accrington & Rossendale College [2004] IRLR 224

Key Facts

All part-time lecturers were dismissed by the college. Two-thirds of them were women. The college then rehired them through an agency. The women were paid less and lost pension rights and other benefits. One of the women brought an action under Art 119 (now Art 157) TFEU and named a male full-timer as a comparator.

Key Law

The ECJ held that there was no possible action under Art 119 since the employer was now different rather than the same or an associated employer as required.

➡ Key Links

Lawrence and Others v North Yorkshire County Council C-320/00 [2002] ECR I-7325 where the same applied to cleaners working for tendered private companies.

(ECJ) Macarthys Ltd v Smith [1980] ICR 672

Key Facts

A stockroom manageress learnt that a male employee who she had replaced had received significantly higher wages for the job. She claimed equal pay. The English court held that there was no claim as there was no contemporaneous male in the same employment.

Key Law

The ECJ held that comparison could be made with any male doing the same work for the same or an associated employer and there was no need for contemporaneous employment. However, it did state that a hypothetical male comparator could not be used. The Advocate-General in his reasoned opinion also suggested that 'equal work' could include jobs with a high degree of similarity while not exactly the same.

Key Links

Diocese of Hallam Trustees v Connaughten [1996] 3 CMLR 93 where HL applied the same principle to a female employee using the male who took over her job at much higher pay as a comparator.

(HL) Rainey v Greater Glasgow Health Board [1987] ICR 129

Key Facts

The employer advertised for a prosthetics technician when there was a shortage of skilled staff in the area. As a result it hired a man who had been in the private sector on more than the usual rate of pay in the public sector. His pay was greater than women employees working for the board who then claimed equal pay.

Key Law

The court held that the shortage of qualified staff and the need to recruit from the private sector was a genuine material factor justifying the difference in pay.

(ECJ) Enderby v Frenchay Health Authority [1994] ICR 112

Key Facts

A woman who had worked for the health authority for six years claimed equal pay with a male comparator who had only been employed by it for one year.

Key Law

It was held that she was entitled to the pay increments that the man would have been awarded if he had the same service as her.

(ECJ) Handels-og Kontorfunktionaernes Forbund i Danmark v Dansk Arbejdsgiverforening (acting for Danfoss) [1991] ICR 74

Key Facts

A Danish trade union challenged pay rate criteria set by the Danish Employers Association and how they had been applied by an employer, Danfoss. The criteria included flexibility and seniority but, though the minimum pay for each grade was the same for both men and women, nevertheless the average pay for women within each grade was lower than for that of men.

Key Law

The ECJ held that, even though neutral criteria for setting pay might appear non-discriminatory at first sight, if the criteria could be shown to result in systematic discrimination this could only be because the employer applied the criteria in a discriminatory manner.

Cadman v Health and Safety Executive [2006] ICR 1623

Key Facts

Mrs Cadman worked for the Health & Safety Executive (HSE) from 1990, and by 2001 was head of a unit on an annual salary of £35,000. She complained that four male colleagues, in the same pay band, earned between £39,000 and £44,000. The men all had longer service which the HSE used to justify the pay differential. She argued a breach of Art 141 (now Art 157) TFEU.

Key Law

The ECJ held that different lengths of experience could justify different pay rates for otherwise similar jobs, although this was not conclusive. It would not be so 'where the worker provides evidence capable of giving rise to serious doubts as to whether ... the criterion of length of service is, in the circumstances, appropriate'.

Key Judgment

The court explained that *'rewarding ... experience acquired which enables the worker to perform his duties better constitutes a legitimate objective of pay policy. As a general rule ... the criterion of length of service is appropriate to attain that objective. Length of service goes hand in hand with experience, and experience generally enables the worker to perform his duties better'*.

Key Comment

The case clearly demonstrates that, while incremental pay scales can be justified on the basis that length of experience may indicate better ability to do the job, too many increments may be both unjustified and potentially discriminatory.

Bilka Kaufhaus GmbH v Weber von Hartz [1987] ICR 110

 Key Facts

Harz was employed by a large department store for ten years full-time and then part-time. Only 10 per cent of male employees were part-time compared to 27.7 per cent of women. Harz complained that the occupational pension scheme was only available to employees who had worked full-time for 15 of the last 20 years and so she was excluded. The store admitted that it deliberately discriminated against part-time workers but argued that this was a genuine need of the business because part-timers were less likely to be prepared to work late afternoons and Saturdays.

 Key Law

The ECJ held that this could amount to indirect discrimination. While the provision was neutral it could affect women more because of the much larger percentage of part-time females. It also accepted occupational pension schemes as pay. The ECJ held that national courts should decide whether there is a real need to apply different rules for part-timers, but that there must be objective justification for doing so based on the following criteria:

- The measure must correspond to a genuine need of the business
- It must be suitable for obtaining the objective
- It must be necessary for that purpose.

 Key Comment

In the event the national court decided that there was no objective justification for the discrimination.

 Hayward v Camell Laird Shipbuilders Ltd (No 2) [1988] ICR 464

 Key Facts

Julie Hayward was a cook working for Cammell Laird Shipbuilders and was paid a lower rate of pay than many skilled male workers in the factory. However, she did enjoy certain benefits that they did not which included better sickness pay, paid meal breaks and better holidays. An independent job evaluation survey had concluded that her work was of equal value to her male comparators. As a result she claimed equal pay with three named male comparators – a painter, a thermal engineer and a joiner. Her claim for equal pay for work of value was in fact the first ever to be heard in the UK.

Key Law

The tribunal rejected her claim explaining that, taken as a whole, her conditions were not less favourable than her male comparators. As such it held that pay was not the only consideration but that other terms and conditions in the contract must be taken into account in determining the outcome. The House of Lords (now the Supreme Court), however, rejected this approach and held that each and every term of the contract should be compared and be equal, not that the terms should not be overall less favourable. On this basis if there is a difference in pay it should be adjusted which would otherwise be to deny the women her rights under EU law in Art 119 (now Art 157) TFEU.

Key Judgment

Lord Goff commented: *'This may, in some cases, lead to what has been called mutual enhancement or leap-frogging, as terms of the woman's contract and the man's contract are both ... upgraded to bring them into line with each other ... if the construction ... does not accord with the true intention of Parliament, then the appropriate course ... is to amend the legislation to bring it into line with its true intention. In the meantime, however, the decision ... may have the salutary effect of drawing to the attention of employers and trade unions the absolute need for ensuring that the pay structures for the different groups of employees do not contain any element of sex discrimination.'*

Key Comment

The case highlighted the conflict that had existed between the Equal Pay Act 1970 and EU law under Directive 75/117 (now in the Recast Directive 2006/54). This had led to the UK being found in breach of its EU law obligations in case 61/81 and had led to the Equal Pay (Amendment) Regulations 1983 and the insertion of a provision for equal pay for equal value which was not in the original Act.

(ECJ) Barber v Guardian Royal Exchange [1990] ICR 616

Key Facts

Barber was made redundant when he was 52. His employer paid him the statutory redundancy payment but would not pay him an early retirement pension under the contracted out scheme as this was only available to men over the age of 55 when made redundant. By contrast women in similar circumstances were eligible for the early pension scheme at age 50. Barber argued that this was a breach of Art 119 (now Art 157) TFEU.

Key Law

The ECJ held that money paid out under such schemes was pay for the purposes of the Article and so there was an unjustified breach. The court also held that the nature of the scheme was irrelevant. Occupational pension schemes would come within the scope of the Article whether they were employer schemes which supplemented the state's retirement scheme (as in *Bilka-Kaufhaus*) or the so-called 'contracted out' schemes as was the case here.

Key Judgment

The court stated that: '*Although it is true that many advantages granted by an employer also reflect considerations of social policy, the fact that a benefit is in the nature of pay cannot be called into question where the worker is entitled to receive the benefit in question from the employer by reason of the existence of the employment relationship.*'

Key Comment

Because of the potential effects on contracted out schemes, the court decided that its ruling would not be applied retrospectively. The case, in any case, led to a flood of preliminary rulings, mainly from the UK and the Netherlands.

Worringham & Humphries v Lloyds Bank Ltd 69/80 [1981] ECR 767

 Key Facts

The bank gave supplementary payments to male employees under the age of 25 towards contributions to an occupational pension scheme. It made no such payments towards female employees of the same age and was challenged by female employees as being a breach of Art 119 (now Art 157) TFEU.

Key Law

The ECJ held that sums included in calculating an employee's gross salary which are used to directly determine the calculation of other benefits such as redundancy payment, family credit, etc. count as pay for the purposes of the Article. Since women under 25 were denied the subsidy this was a clear breach of Art 119 (now Art 157) TFEU.

6.2 Sex discrimination

 Marshall v Southampton and South West Hampshire AHA (No 1) 152/84 [1986] QB 401

 Key Facts

A woman who was forced to retire by her employer argued that the different retirement ages for men and women in the UK was discrimination under the Equal Treatment Directive 76/207 (now in the Recast Directive 2006/54). The problem was whether the Directive could be enforced through direct effect.

Key Law

The ECJ confirmed that the UK law failed to fully implement the Directive and identified that the woman could only rely on the improperly implemented Directive against her employer because it was the health service, an organ of the state. The court recognised that Directives are only capable of vertical direct effect.

 Key Judgment

The ECJ stated: *'According to [Art 288] ... the binding nature of a Directive ... exists only in relation to "each Member State to which*

it is addressed". It follows that a Directive may not of itself impose obligations on an individual and that a provision of a Directive may not be relied upon as such against such a person.'

(HL) Duke v GEC Reliance Ltd [1988] AC 618

Key Facts

In similar facts to *Marshall*, the claimant did not wish to retire at the required age at the time under UK law. However, in contrast to *Marshall* the woman was employed by a private company, not by the state.

Key Law

The House of Lords (now the Supreme Court) held that it was not bound to apply Directive 76/207 (now in the Recast Directive 2006/54) because Directives are not horizontally directly effective. Despite the UK being at fault for failing to fully implement the Directive, the availability of a remedy then was entirely dependent on the identity of the employer. It also rejected a request to apply the principle of indirect effect from *Von Colson* and would not make a reference for a preliminary ruling on the issue because it claimed the principle of direct effect was settled law.

Key Problem

The case shows that the availability of a remedy for a right given in a Directive is dependent on the nature of the party against whom the action is being brought. So it results in arbitrary justice.

Key Comment

The case appears to be one that would have been perfectly suited to the indirect effect process. Obviously it would be unfair to in effect punish individuals for the failure of their Member State to implement or to properly implement EU law. Here there would have been no such punishment since it would have only involved keeping the woman on past the normal retirement age for women at the time.

(EAT) Grieg v Community Industry [1979] IRLR 158

Key Facts

Two women were offered posts in a painting and decorating team. On the first day one of the women failed to turn up for work so the employer dismissed the woman who did because he felt it would be uncomfortable for her to be the only female on an all-male team.

Key Law

This was held to be direct discrimination. The fact that it was done for a worthy motive was irrelevant.

(EAT) Saunders v Richmond-upon-Thames London Borough Council [1978] ICR 75

Key Facts

A female golfer attended an interview for a position as a professional golfer. She was asked numerous questions that on the surface appeared to discriminate such as whether she was trying to blaze a trail for women, what she thought the frequency of women being appointed as professional golfers was, etc. When she was informed that she had not been appointed she claimed that this was due to discrimination in the questioning that she had been subjected to.

Key Law

The EAT identified that there may be practical reasons for asking such questions and gave the example of a man being interviewed for a position as a headteacher in a girls' school being asked questions about his ability to relate to girls. As a result the asking of such questions was not discriminatory.

Key Comment

One other interesting point raised by the EAT was the possibility that making such questions unlawful might actually make it difficult to show discrimination in interview situations since a prejudiced employer would be less likely to show his real prejudice.

(EAT) Price v Civil Service Commission [1983] ICR 428

Key Facts

At the time the Civil Service had a scheme of direct entry at Executive Officer level for applicants with certain qualifications. An advertisement stated that only people between the ages of 17 and 28 were eligible to apply in such a way. The claimant argued that this was discrimination as she was prevented from applying.

Key Law

It was held that this was indirect discrimination. Although the requirement applied irrespective of gender, because of childcare arrangements fewer women would be able to comply.

(CA) Hardys & Hansons plc v Lax [2005] IRLR 726

Key Facts

The claimant was employed as a retail recruitment manager for a brewery. She went on maternity leave and asked if she could return to work on a part-time basis and the employer refused justifying this on the basis that there was an operational need for full-time employees. She claimed indirect discrimination. The tribunal had found with her as it felt that there was no real difficulty in the circumstances in allowing her to work part-time. The employer appealed arguing that the tribunal should have applied the 'reasonable range of responses' test (see Chapter 9).

Key Law

The appeal rejected the employer's view that the tribunal was bound only by the 'reasonable range of responses' test. It concluded that the tribunal was entitled also to make its judgment based on the strength of the justification presented by the employer, the burden being on the employer to show that the decision (here not to allow the claimant to work part-time) is objectively justified despite its discriminatory effect.

Key Judgment

Pill LJ explained: '*The principle of proportionality requires the tribunal to take into account the reasonable needs of the business. But it has to make its own judgment, upon a fair and detailed analysis of the working practices and business considerations involved, as to whether the proposal is reasonable necessary.*'

(ECJ) Johnston v Chief Constable of the Royal Ulster Constabulary [1987] ICR 83

Key Facts

A female officer in the Royal Ulster Constabulary argued that not issuing firearms to female officers was a breach of the right of equal treatment under Directive 76/207 (now in the Recast Directive 2006/54) and in effect acted as a bar to promotion for female officers. The RUC claimed that its policy was justified on public safety and national security grounds and was also authorised by a statutory instrument. It also argued that allowing women to carry arms increased their risk of becoming targets for assassination and that the derogation Art 2(2) of Directive 76/207 would apply.

Key Law

The ECJ held that there was no general public safety exemption in the Directive and that the only derogation available was that in Art 2 on occupational activities which by nature required that the sex of the worker is a determining factor. It held that the derogation should be applied strictly but accepted that the principle of proportionality should also be applied. The policy could fall within the derogation because of the politically sensitive situation then in Northern Ireland.

Key Problem

The ECJ recognised that the effect of the certificate was to deprive female officers of the right to a judicial hearing or indeed any remedy. As such it was a breach of human rights.

(CA) Smith v Safeways Stores [1996] IRLR 456

Key Facts

Company rules required that male employees should have 'tidy hair not below collar length and no unconventional styles'. The claimant, who worked in the delicatessen, had long hair and wore it in a ponytail. He was dismissed for refusing to get his hair cut and claimed direct discrimination since female employees were allowed to have long hair. He initially succeeded in his claim but his employer then appealed successfully against the decision.

Key Law

The Court of Appeal held that the dress code was not discriminatory merely because it took 'a conventional outlook'.

Key Judgment

Phillips LJ explained that: *'Rules concerning appearance will not be discriminatory because their content is different for men and women if they enforce a common principle of smartness or conventionality, and taken as a whole and not garment by garment or item by item, neither gender is treated less favourably in enforcing that principle.'*

Key Problem

The judgment would appear to be based on a value judgment of what constitutes smartness and convention rather than on an objective standard applied regardless of gender.

Stewart v Cleveland Guest Engineering Ltd [1994] IRLR 440

Key Facts

Here men in a factory posted pin-ups of nude females from magazines and calendars on the walls. The female claimant took offence and objected at the practice to management. They initially ordered that they be removed but then reversed their decision when they were approached by other workers who claimed that they did not object. The claimant then argued that she had been sexually harassed by the behaviour.

Key Law

The EAT held that there was no harassment since the materials could be considered as gender neutral: men as well as women might be offended and therefore any alleged discrimination based on sex did not exist.

Key Comment

The judgment would seem to miss the point. The nude pictures were of women and therefore it is arguable whether there was any gender neutrality, the judges merely created a situation in which women might arguably feel more vulnerable.

Key Problem

The case demonstrates the problem originally faced by women trying to bring sexual harassment claims. Since there was no actual law on the issue women had to bring claims under the old s 6(2)(b) Sex Discrimination Act 1975 that they had suffered 'any other detriment'. As they both had to prove that they had been treated less favourably than a man in the same position and show that they had suffered a detriment they had difficulty in succeeding in such circumstances. As there is now a definition of harassment in the Equality Act 2010 it is unlikely that cases such as this will survive.

(EAT) Insitu Cleaning Co Ltd v Heads [1995] IRLR 4

Key Facts

A manager remarked to a female supervisor at a management meeting regarding the size of her breasts. She argued discrimination.

Key Law

It was held that she had been subjected to a detriment under the then s 6(2)(b) Sex Discrimination Act 1975. The court did comment that she could have used internal grievance procedure rather than commencing proceedings immediately.

(EAT) Bracebridge Engineering Ltd v Darby [1990] IRLR 3

Key Facts

The claimant was subjected to a single indecent assault. The issues for the court were whether this amounted to discrimination and whether the employer was vicariously liable.

Key Law

The court held that a single act can amount to harassment, here because of its serious nature. The employer was liable because, since the perpetrators were involved in disciplinary supervision at the time, their acts were in the course of employment.

(EAT) Wileman v Minilec Engineering Ltd [1988] IRLR 144

Key Facts

The claimant complained of harassment by a company director. This included sexual remarks such as a suggestion that she should go topless, as well as being rubbed up against him. The law at that time (s 6(2)(b) of the Sexual Discrimination Act 1975) required her to show that she had suffered a detriment. The company argued that she had not since she had posed in flimsy clothing for a newspaper and would be unaffected by his behaviour.

Key Law

The court held that, while she might be happy to accept sexual remarks from one person, this may not apply in the case of others and the newspaper picture was irrelevant. She had been discriminated against.

6.3 Gender reassignment and sexual orientation

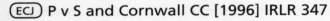

(ECJ) P v S and Cornwall CC [1996] IRLR 347

Key Facts

A male employee at a Cornwall college informed the Director of Studies that he was to undergo 'gender reassignment' to become a woman and that this involved a period of dressing and behaving like a woman and ultimately surgery for a full sex change. He was later dismissed and claimed that this was unlawful sexual discrimination and therefore a breach of Directive 76/207.

Key Law

The issue before the ECJ was whether dismissal of a transsexual was in fact for reasons of gender as it in effect concerned both genders. The court held that the whole purpose of the Directive was to prevent discrimination and promote equality – a fundamental principle of law to be applied universally. It thus rejected the argument raised by the British government that the dismissal was not discriminatory since it could have equally have applied to a female and to a male transsexual. The transsexual was being discriminated against by being treated less favourably than a person of the sex to whom he/she had belonged prior to the gender reassignment.

(CA) Chief Constable of Yorkshire v A [2005] AC 51

Key Facts

The issue was whether the claimant could be classified under the changed gender.

Key Law

The court held that under the Gender Recognition Act 2004, once a person has undergone gender reassignment and gained formal recognition under the Act they are entitled to be treated as a person of the acquired gender.

English v Thomas Sanderson Blinds Ltd [2009] IRLR 206

CA

Key Facts

The claimant had been taunted for years by colleagues who called him gay because he had attended public school and lived in Brighton. In fact he was not gay and he knew that his work colleagues did not actually think that he was.

Key Law

It was held that the abuse amounted to discrimination and he was covered by the Sexual Orientation Regulations despite not being gay.

6.4 Race discrimination

West Midlands Passenger Transport Executive v Singh [1988] ICR 614

CA

Key Facts

The claimant was Sikh and had worked as an inspector for WMPTE for 11 years. He was rejected in an application for promotion to one of 13 senior inspector posts. He claimed discrimination and sought disclosure of the qualifications and experience and significantly the ethnicity of all 55 applicants. The employer agreed to disclose this but refused to provide the same information for all positions advertised in the same grade bands between 1983 when an equal opportunities policy had been implemented and the time of his application in 1985.

Key Law

On appeal the court held that it is possible to have discovery of statistical evidence relating to the engagement and promotion of different ethnicity and race since this might reveal discrimination. The material could be relevant in that (i) it may reveal that treatment of different races was an effective cause for them not receiving promotion, and

(ii) it might enable the employee to counter an argument by an employer that it was operating an effective equal opportunities policy.

Key Judgment

Balcombe LJ explained: *'The suitability of candidates can rarely be measured objectively; often subjective judgments will be made. If there is evidence of a high percentage rate of failure to achieve promotion at particular levels by members of a particular racial group, this may indicate that the real reason for refusal is a conscious or unconscious racial attitude which involves stereotyped assumptions about members of that group.'*

Lambeth LBC v Commission for Racial Equality [1990] ICR 768

CA

Key Facts

A local council was reserving posts in its housing benefits department for Afro-Caribbean and Asian applicants because the jobs were basically managerial in character.

Key Law

The court rejected the argument that this was appropriate since the positions did not involve personal service promoting the welfare of a particular racial group and therefore had no justifiable occupational requirement.

CA Jones v Tower Boot Co Ltd [1997] IRLR 168

Key Facts

The claimant, a 16-year-old of mixed race, started work in a shoe factory and from the start he was subjected to both verbal and physical racial abuse. This included being called 'chimp' and 'monkey', being whipped on the legs and even burnt with a hot screwdriver. After four weeks he could take no more and left, claiming racial harassment. The employer argued that the actions of the boy's colleagues were not in the course of their employment since they were not authorised and alternatively that it had done everything possible to stop the acts.

Key Law

The appeal focused on whether the abuse took place in the course of employment. The court held that common law principles of vicarious liability should not be used in such a way as to defeat the purposes of the legislation on racial equality and that the words 'in the course of employment' should be used in a way that laymen understood them. The employer was liable.

Brown v TNT Express Worldwide (UK) Ltd [2001] ICR 182

CA

Key Facts

An employee asked for time off work to see an adviser about a discrimination claim that he was considering bringing and was refused despite the fact that requests for time off for personal reasons were usually granted. He took the time off anyway and was dismissed.

Key Law

It was held that the dismissal amounted to victimisation. It rejected the employer's argument that the only relevant comparator would have been one who had brought a claim against the employer but not under the Race Relations Act.

Chief Constable of West Yorkshire Police v Khan [2001] IRLR 830
HL

Key Facts

A police officer had applied for promotion and his application had not been supported so he made a claim for racial discrimination. He then applied for a promotion with another police force. When his Chief Constable failed to provide him with a reference he claimed victimisation.

Key Law

His claim failed since the Chief Constable's failure to provide a reference was not because of the proceedings that the claimant had brought but so as not to prejudice his position in those proceedings.

R v Commission for Racial Equality ex p Westminster City Council [1985] IRLR 426
CA

Key Facts

A black claimant had been given a temporary appointment. This was then withdrawn when other workers were threatening industrial action if his employment continued.

Key Law

It was held that the then Commission for Racial Equality could issue a non-discrimination notice to the employer. Without such enforcement the legislation would have been unworkable.

(CA) Panesar v Nestle & Co [1980] IRLR 64

Key Facts

A Sikh employee in a factory producing chocolate complained that a rule that employees should not wear long hair or beards discriminated against him. He argued that he was unable to comply with the rule because his religion required him to have both.

Key Law

The court accepted that the rule did discriminate indirectly since it was a condition applying to the whole workforce but having an adverse effect on Sikhs. Nevertheless the claim failed because the court accepted that there were valid health and safety and hygiene reasons for the rule and so it was justified.

(EAT) Tottenham Green Under Fives' Centre v Marshall [1991] IRLR 162

Key Facts

A day centre for Afro-Caribbean children had a policy maintaining an ethnic balance between its staff and the children in its care. It advertised for a position open to Afro-Caribbean workers only.

Key Law

It was held that the centre was able to rely on a genuine occupational requirement under what was then s 5 of the Race Relations Act 1975, of provision of welfare services to a particular racial group.

6.5 Disability discrimination

(EAT) Chief Constable of Dumfries & Galloway v Adams [2009] IRLR 612

Key Facts

A police officer had ME, a debilitating condition causing chronic fatigue. He complained when he suffered mobility problems while working on night shift.

Key Law

Since night shift could be construed as a normal day-to-day activity because a number of employees are subject to such requirements, the police officer was held to be disabled for the purposes of the Disability Discrimination Act 1995.

 Power v Panasonic UK Ltd [2003] IRLR 151

Key Facts

An area sales manager had the area that she was responsible for considerably enlarged. She then suffered from stress resulting in a lengthy sickness absence and was dismissed. It was accepted that during that absence she was both depressed and drinking heavily.

Key Law

The tribunal concerned itself with what came first, the drinking or the depression, in determining cause. The EAT said that this was not necessary to consider cause, merely whether there was an impairment within the meaning of the then Disability Discrimination Act 1995.

Key Comment

The principle is likely to fit in within the Equality Act 2010.

 Kenny v Hampshire Constabulary [1999] IRLR 76

Key Facts

Kenny suffered from cerebral palsy and needed assistance to go to the toilet. He was originally offered employment but this was then withdrawn when it was found that the necessary type of assistance was not available and would have to be provided by the employer.

Key Law

It was held that, while employees may be under an obligation to make reasonable adjustments, this does not extend as far as having to provide for personal needs.

Key Comment

The case was heard under the Disability Discrimination Act 1995 which was much more restrictive in the case of disability than the Equality Act 2010. However, the principle in the case probably survives the new Act. Employers are only obliged to make reasonable adjustments; providing in effect an additional employee as a kind of carer for Kenny would have been financially prohibitive.

(EAT) Kapadia v Lambeth LBC [2000] IRLR 699

Key Facts
Kapadia claimed that he was disabled through reactive depression and that this affected his day-to-day activities. He was subjected to a medical examination by his employer's doctor but he then refused to authorise disclosure of the report to his employer.

Key Law
At the tribunal he was not affected because his symptoms were controlled by medication. The employer argued that Kapadia had failed to prove that he was disabled, and the tribunal agreed. The EAT disagreed as it was sufficient that he could show an impairment, not that it had to be present during trial. It did comment that he should have disclosed the report.

(EAT) Farmiloe v Lane Group plc [2004] PIQR P22

Key Facts
A warehouse worker who suffered from psoriasis could not wear safety boots as a result. A health and safety officer insisted that he wear them and threatened him with disciplinary action if he did not. The employer approached footwear manufacturers who were unable to produce suitable footwear so he was dismissed as there was no other suitable alternative work.

Key Law
It was held that health and safety law overrode disability discrimination. The employer had gone to great lengths in an attempt to make reasonable adjustments so the dismissal was fair.

(CA) Meikle v Nottinghamshire County Council [2004] EWCA Civ 859

Key Facts
A school teacher who suffered from deteriorating vision eventually lost the sight in one eye and had only limited

vision in the other. She was given a timetable of classes that she needed to teach each day and found it difficult to read and asked for one in larger print, but this was never done. She was also made to teach in a classroom some distance from her normal classroom and she asked if this could be changed to make it easier to get to her class, but again this did not happen. She also asked for extra preparation time for her classes, again with no response. She had to take time off due to eye strain and eventually claimed constructive dismissal.

Key Law

It was held that the school had failed to make reasonable adjustments. There was nothing excessive or costly in the adjustments that had been asked for. She had therefore been unfairly dismissed.

 Secretary of State for Works and Pensions (Job Centre Plus) v Wilson [2010] UKEAT 0289 09 1902

Key Facts

The claimant who suffered from panic attacks and anxiety was redeployed to another office when the job centre in which she worked was closed. The old office was very near to her home and had involved no travel. She asked her employer to allow her to work from home and stated that this was the only basis on which she was prepared to work. She was dismissed after taking sick leave.

Key Law

The EAT, reversing the tribunal decision, upheld the dismissal. It was not practicable to allow the claimant to work from home and refusing to work at the new office made reasonable adjustments impossible.

6.6 Discrimination on religion and belief

 Grainger Ltd v Nicholson [2010] IRLR 10

Key Facts

The claimant was selected for redundancy. He argued that this was in fact an unfair dismissal. He claimed that the dismissal was discriminatory and contrary to the Employment Equality (Religion or Belief) Regulations 2003 and that it was due to his expressed belief that climate change was man-made. The issue was whether or not such beliefs could fall under the regulations.

Key Law

The court held that, provided such beliefs were genuinely held, they could be classed as a 'philosophical belief' for the purposes of the regulations. The EAT explained the criteria for determining what a belief is:

(a) it must be genuinely held

(b) it must not merely be an opinion based on fact

(c) it must be a belief involving a weighty aspect of human life and behaviour

(d) it must be cogent and have some importance

(e) it must be worthy in a democratic society, not incompatible with human dignity and not conflict with basic human rights.

Ladele v London Borough of Lambeth [2009] EWCA Civ 1357

CA

Key Facts

A registrar was dismissed after refusing to marry same-sex couples. She was a committed Christian and argued that she had refused to follow the council's equality-for-all policy because it offended her religious beliefs.

Key Law

The court identified that the dismissal was not on the grounds of religion but was a straightforward breach of her contractual obligations. The court also noted that the Sexual Orientation Regulations 2007 took precedence over her right to practise her religious beliefs since this involved her doing so in a discriminatory fashion.

Azmi v Kirklees Metropolitan Borough Council [2007] IRLR 484

 Key Facts

A Muslim teaching assistant in a primary school complained that a rule preventing her from wearing a full-face veil was discrimination on grounds of religion.

Key Law

It was held that this was not direct discrimination since any woman teacher would have been subjected to the same dress code regardless of her religion. Neither was it indirect discrimination since the dress code was a necessary and proportionate means of achieving a legitimate aim that children of such a young age should have a full facial view of their teachers.

 Eweida v British Airways [2010] IRLR 322

 Key Facts

A female employee claimed that a rule preventing her from wearing a cross outside of her uniform to identify her Christian beliefs was indirect discrimination on religious grounds. She also compared herself with a Sikh who might be permitted to wear a turban.

 Key Law

It was held that there was no indirect discrimination and that the two situations were not comparable. In the case of the Sikh this could be seen as a doctrinal religious requirement whereas there is no such doctrinal requirement in the Christian religion for wearing a cross.

Glasgow City Council v McNab [2007] IRLR 476

 Key Facts

A teacher applied for a position in pastoral care in a Roman Catholic school and was rejected and not even interviewed because he was not a Catholic. He claimed discrimination and the school argued that the requirement for employees to be Catholic was a genuine occupational requirement.

Key Law
It was held that, while the school was a faith school, it was not a necessary requirement that the teacher should be of Catholic faith. There was no occupational requirement in the circumstances and the school's actions were unlawful discrimination.

6.7 Age discrimination

(ECJ) **Wolf v Stadt Frankfurt am Main [2010] IRLR 244**

Key Facts
The claimant argued that the policy that applicants for the fire service must be under the age of 30 was discriminatory.

Key Law
The court held that the requirement was a genuine occupational requirement. It was accepted that fire fighting and rescue duties were traditionally carried out by younger officers so that unlimited recruitment would limit the number of officers who could engage in such duties.

(EAT) **London Borough of Tower Hamlets v Wooster [2009] IRLR 980**

Key Facts
The claimant had been made redundant at age 49. He was able to show evidence that the decision to make him redundant rather than to redeploy him was so that the employer could avoid him becoming eligible for an early retirement scheme.

Key Law
It was held that this was direct discrimination as the only reason for the claimant's dismissal was in effect his age.

6.8 Discrimination on trade union grounds

(EAT) Harrison v Kent County Council [1995] ICR 434

Key Facts

The claimant, also a trade union representative, had formerly led a lengthy industrial dispute in his employment which was also quite hostile and bitter at times. He left that employment and applied for another position but was not successful. He argued that the decision not to appoint him was because of his trade union membership and therefore unlawful under s 137 of the Trade Union and Labour Relations (Consolidation) Act 1992.

Key Law

The EAT held that there was a significant overlap between trade union membership and trade union activity and therefore not being given the position could have been based on his trade union membership.

 Key Link

Associated British Ports v Palmer [1995] IRLR 399 which in effect gives a different answer.

(HL) Associated British Ports v Palmer [1995] IRLR 399

Key Facts

The employer had redrafted individual contracts in replacement of a previous collective agreement. This was challenged as unlawful.

Key Law

The Court of Appeal had originally stated that the process discriminated against trade union rights. The House of Lords (now the Supreme Court) overruled this and held that the purpose was flexibility and it was therefore lawful.

(CA) Bass Taverns Ltd v Burgess [1995] IRLR 595

Key Facts
The employee was the manager of a public house and a shop steward of a relevant trade union. He was also a trainer for the brewery, for which he received an additional fee. During one training session in which he was entitled to make a brief presentation about the union he was critical of the brewery and suggested that it only cared about its profits, not about the welfare of its managers. The brewery objected to this and withdrew his post as a trainer. He claimed constructive dismissal arguing that this was because of his legitimate trade union activities.

Key Law
The court held that there was an implied term that the presentation would not be used to criticise the employer and that his actions took him outside of the context of legitimate trade union activity.

(CA) Marley Tile Co Ltd v Shaw [1980] IRLR 25

Key Facts
The employee became a shop steward for a group of workers despite only having been in the company for two months. When he raised an issue with management he was informed that he was not recognised because of his short service. He then called his district official and held a meeting during work's time and was dismissed. He complained that this was unfair dismissal as it was due to legitimate trade union activities.

Key Law
It was held that there was no implied term in the contract that employees could be called to a meeting during work's time so the dismissal was lawful and not unfair.

 Key Links
Zucker v Astrid Jewels Ltd [1978] ICR 1088 EAT

7

Common Law Health and Safety at Work Protection

Common law health and safety at work

Smith v Baker (1891)
An employee does not consent to harm caused during his employment unless he is fully aware of the risk, exercised free choice and voluntarily accepted the risk

Wilsons & Clyde Coal Co Ltd v English (1938)
The employer owes a non-delegable duty of care to provide safe colleagues, plant and equipment, premises, and systems of work

Sutherland v Hatton and Others (2002)
And now has a duty to protect the employee's psychiatric health if he is aware of the employee's susceptibility to stress so that the injury is foreseeable

HL Smith v Baker [1891] AC 325

Key Facts

A quarry worker was injured when a conveyor carrying rocks over his head faltered and some fell on him. He had already complained that the practice was dangerous and the defendant argued that, by continuing to work, he had voluntarily accepted the risk of harm.

Key Law

The defence failed. The court held that the workman had only consented to general dangers relating to his work. He could not be said to have accepted the risk of the specific harm suffered which was involuntary.

Key Judgment

Lord Halsbury LC explained: '*A person who relies on the maxim must shew a consent to the particular thing done … It appears to me that the proposition upon which the defendants must rely must be a far wider one than is involved in the maxim.*'

CA Roles v Nathan [1963] 1 WLR 1117

Key Facts

Two chimney sweeps, cleaning flues in a factory, died after inhaling fumes. They had been warned by the factory owners of the danger of working in the chimney while the furnace was lit but had ignored the advice.

Key Law

The court held that the factory owner, as occupier of the premises, is entitled to assume that professional visitors will guard against risks that are within their professional knowledge. The claim failed.

QBD O'Reilly v National Rail & Tramway Appliances [1966] 1 All ER 499

Key Facts

Labourers breaking up a disused railway line found what they believed to be an unexploded shell from the Second World War. It was about nine inches long and one inch in diameter. The claimant was injured when he followed the suggestion of work colleagues that he hit the object with a sledgehammer. One had said 'Hit it: what are you scared of?'.

Key Law

The court held that the employer should avoid liability for the negligence of his employees. An employer does owe a duty to provide safe working colleagues. However, in the circumstances the employer had no idea that his employees would behave in such a mindless way and could not be held responsible.

HL Wilsons & Clyde Coal Co Ltd v English [1938] AC 57

Key Facts

A miner was injured due to negligent maintenance of the pit. The owners tried to avoid liability by arguing that they had delegated their responsibilities and liability under various industrial safety laws to their colliery manager by contractually making him entirely responsible for safety.

Key Law

The court held the colliers liable on the basis that their personal liability could not be delegated to a third party, who was in any case an employee. The court also indicated the scope of the duty: to provide competent working colleagues; safe plant and equipment; a safe place of work; and a safe system of work.

(CA) Bux v Slough Metals [1974] 1 All ER 262

Key Facts

An employee was provided with safety goggles in compliance with health and safety regulations but refused to use them because he claimed that they misted up. The employer was aware of this. The employee was then injured by a splash of molten metal.

Key Law

The court held that the employer was liable for failing to ensure that the goggles were worn. It identified that the duty is not just to provide safe working systems but to ensure that they are followed.

 Key Links

Pape v Cumbria CC [1992] 3 All ER 211 where there was breach of a duty to warn that not wearing gloves could lead to dermatitis.

(HL) Coltman v Bibby Tankers [1988] AC 276

Key Facts

An employee was injured because of a defect in the hull of a ship and claimed for his injuries.

Key Law

The Court of Appeal held that the injury was not actionable because it fell outside of the statutory definition of 'equipment'. The House of Lords (now the Supreme Court) reversed the decision and accepted that the definition within the Act could include the hull in the circumstances of the case.

Walker v Northumberland County Council [1995] 1 All ER 737

QBD

Key Facts

A senior social worker suffered a nervous breakdown as a result of work-related stress. On returning to work he was promised that his workload would reduce in a return-to-work agreement. In fact he was faced with a huge backlog of work built up during his absence. As a result he suffered a second breakdown causing him to leave work permanently after he was dismissed on sickness grounds. His claim was successful. Leave for an appeal to the Court of Appeal was granted but the case was settled beforehand for £175,000.

Key Law

The court held that the employer was liable because after the first breakdown it was aware of his susceptibility to stress and did nothing to reduce his workload or the pressure associated with it. It had thus placed him under even more stressful conditions.

Key Judgment

As Colman J explained: *'It is clear law that an employer has a duty to provide his employee with a safe system of work and to take reasonable steps to protect him from risks which are reasonably foreseeable ... there is no logical reason why risk of psychiatric damage should be excluded from the ... duty.'*

Key Comment

The case is significant in that it expanded the duty owed by employers to employees to include their psychiatric welfare.

Sutherland v Hatton and Others [2002] EWCA Civ 76

CA

Key Facts

This case was in fact a number of joint appeals on stress-related illnesses at work. Two claimants were teachers; one was a local authority administrator; and one was a factory worker. All were claiming that they were forced to stop work because of stress-related psychiatric illnesses caused by their employers.

Key Law

The appeals were decided on whether the injuries were foreseeable but the court also issued important guidelines on stress claims:

- The basic principles of negligence must apply including the usual principles of employers' liability;
- The critical question for the court to answer is whether the type of harm suffered was foreseeable;
- Foreseeability depends on what the reasonable employer knew or ought reasonably to have known;
- An employer can assume that an employee can cope with the normal pressures of the work unless the employer has specific knowledge that an employee has a particular problem;
- The same test should apply whatever the employment;
- The employer should take steps to prevent possible harm when possibility of harm would be obvious to a reasonable employer;
- The employer will be liable if he then fails to take steps that are reasonable in the circumstances to avoid the harm;
- The nature of the employment, the employer's available resources, the counselling and treatment services provided are all relevant in determining whether the employer has taken effective steps to avoid the harm, and in any case the employer is only expected to take steps that will do some good;
- The employee must show that the employer's breach of duty caused the harm not merely that the harm is stress-related;
- Where there is more than one cause of the harm the employer will only be liable for that portion of damages that relates to the harm actually caused by his/her breach of duty;
- Damages should take account of any pre-existing disorder.

Key Comment

Andrew Collender QC [in *Stress in the workplace* New Law Journal 22nd February 2003, pp 248 and 250] discusses a problem recognised by the court: 'whilst it is possible to identify some jobs that are intrinsically physically dangerous, it is rather more difficult to identify which jobs are intrinsically so stressful that physical or psychological harm is to be expected more often than in other jobs'.

→ **Key Link**

Barber v Somerset CC [2004] UKHL 13 which was a further appeal to HL from one of the appeals in *Hatton*.

Ginty v Belmont Building Supplies Ltd [1959] 1 All ER 414
(QBD)

Key Facts

An employee was injured after slipping from a roof on which he was working. He claimed for his injuries.

Key Law

The court accepted that the appropriate safety equipment, duckboards, was provided. It was the failure by the claimant to use safety equipment that actually led to injury so the defence of *volenti* applied (a complete defence) and the employer was not liable.

(CA) Jones v Livox Quarries Ltd [1952] 2 QB 608

Key Facts

An employee was injured while he was riding on the towbar of a traxcavator in a collision caused by the defendant's negligent driving. This was despite the fact that the habit had been expressly prohibited by his employer.

Key Law

The court held that, while the employer was vicariously liable for his negligent employee, the employee had contributed to his injury by ignoring safety instructions and so damages were reduced by 5 per cent.

Key Judgment

Lord Denning said: '*Contributory negligence does not depend on a duty of care ... [it] does depend on foreseeability ... as ... negligence requires ... foreseeability of harm to others ... contributory negligence requires ... foreseeability of harm to oneself.*'

Johnstone v Bloomsbury Health Authority [1991] 2 All ER 293

Key Facts

A junior doctor brought an action against his employer, a health authority. He complained that the fact that he was expected as a matter of course to work up to 48 hours' overtime per week and having had to be on call had damaged his general mental health.

Key Law

The court held that there was a breach of a non-excludable implied term in his contract to take reasonable steps to care for his health and safety. The employer could not exclude this implied term by use of the specific express terms in the contract and it was liable.

8

TUPE Transfers

TUPE transfers

Litster v Forth Dry Dock & Engineering Co Ltd (1990)
A redundancy occurring because of a relevant transfer is unfair dismissal

Schmidt v Spar und Leihkasse der Fruheren Amter Bordesholm, Kiel und Cronshagen (1995)
Acquired Rights Directive can apply although there is no transfer of tangible assets and can cover activities that are ancillary to the main activity

Suzen v Zehnake Gebaudereinigung GmbH Kraankenhausservice (1997)
An undertaking must comprise persons, assets, etc. facilitating an economic activity

DJM International Ltd v Nicholas (1996)
All rights including maternity, equal pay and other rights not to be discriminated transfer as well as redundancy and dismissal rights

 HL
Litster v Forth Dry Dock & Engineering Co Ltd [1990] 1 AC 546

Key Facts
An employee was dismissed one hour before a transfer of the business to new owners took place. The employee claimed that he had been unfairly dismissed.

Key Law
The claim would have been ineffective because the old employer had gone out of business. However, the court held that his rights had transferred to the new owner and his action could be pursued against the new owner. The House of Lords considered that if the employee is dismissed by redundancy because of the transfer but without any contractual basis then the dismissal is unfair.

Key Comment
The decision broadened the scope of the regulations significantly. It was said that even if there is an economic, technical or organisational (ETO) reason for the dismissal the employer is still bound to act fairly.

Schmidt v Spar und Leihkasse der Fruheren Amter Bordesholm, Kiel und Cronshagen C-392/92 [1995] 2 CMLR 331

 (ECJ)

Key Facts

The employee was the only cleaner in a branch of a bank. Cleaning duties were then transferred to a firm of contractors. The cleaner refused to accept the terms imposed by the contractors which were inferior to those under her former contract and she was dismissed.

Key Law

The ECJ held that: (i) the mere fact that there was no transfer of tangible assets did not mean that the Acquired Rights Directive could not apply; (ii) whether the business retained its identity was a decisive factor; (iii) the Directive can cover activities (such as here) that are ancillary to the main activity; and (iv) the fact that the activity was only carried out by one person also does not necessarily matter. As such the words 'an organised grouping of employees' in the Directive can sometimes apply to one employee.

Suzen v Zehnake Gebaudereinigung GmbH Kraankenhausservice (C-13/95) [1997] 1 CMLR 768

(ECJ)

Key Facts

This involved the transfer of workers employed under a school cleaning contract from one contract to another.

Key Law

The ECJ held that such an entity could not be reduced to the activity entrusted to it but must comprise persons, assets, etc. facilitating an economic activity. In effect the decision meant that, in the absence of a transfer of the workforce, contracting out of the workforce in a labour-intensive sector could not be covered by the Acquired Rights Directive from which the Transfer of Undertakings (Protection of Employment) (TUPE) rights emanate. Although the court did recognise that 'in certain labour-intensive sectors a group of workers engaged in a joint activity on a permanent basis may constitute an economic entity'.

Key Problem

The case caused much confusion in the area of contracting out.

(CA) Dines v Initial Healthcare Services Ltd [1995] IRLR 336

Key Facts

Cleaners at a hospital who were employed by Initial Health Care Services were affected when the contract for cleaning was put out to competitive tender. A different contractor, Pall Mall, won the contract and the cleaners were then made redundant by Initial. Pall Mall took them on but on far less favourable conditions and they claimed unfair dismissal.

Key Law

The court held that there was a relevant transfer under the then Regulation 8 of TUPE since the services were essentially the same. As a result they should have transferred with the contract, their contractual rights should have been protected and they were unfairly dismissed.

(CA) Morris Angel & Son Ltd v Hollande [1993] IRLR 400

Key Facts

A managing director had a provision within his service contract that he would not within one year of leaving solicit any business from any of the company's clients. The company was then sold to new owners and when the managing director left the new owners sought to enforce the provision against him.

Key Law

The court held that the regulations applied so that the new owners were in effect in the shoes of the former owners and all contractual provisions remained. The new owners were, however, only allowed to enforce the provision in respect of clients of the former owners and not in respect of any of their own existing client base.

(EAT) DJM International Ltd v Nicholas [1996] IRLR 76

Key Facts

Ms Nicholas had worked for the company for many years and was then forced to retire at age 60 in 1992. She was re-engaged on a part-time contract and two months later the business was transferred and she continued working for the new owner. Five months later she bought a claim for discrimination based on her effective dismissal at age 60.

Key Law

Her claim would have been out of time but the tribunal extended the three-month limit to include it. It was accepted by the court that rights such as maternity, equal pay and other rights not to be discriminated against also transfer.

(EAT) G4s Justice Services (UK) Ltd v Anstey [2006] IRLR 588

Key Facts

Two employees were dismissed for gross misconduct and before any hearing of their appeal could be heard the business was transferred. The original employer then heard the appeals and reinstated them but the new employer refused to reinstate them arguing that they were not employed 'immediately before the transfer'.

Key Law

The court held that the successful appeal had overturned the dismissals so that they were employed when the transfer occurred. As a result the new employer was obliged to reinstate them.

(CA) Bernadone v Pall Mall Service Group Ltd [2000] IRLR 76

Key Facts

The employee was trying to claim against the new employer for an industrial injury that he had suffered while he was in the service of the former employer who had transferred the business.

Key Law

It was held that all such rights transfer to the new owner. In any case both employers were required by law to hold compulsory insurance. However, the court identified that this would not necessarily apply to local authorities which may have exemption.

Key Links

Martin v Lancashire County Council [2000] IRLR 76 which was a joined appeal with *Bernadone*. Here the issue was whether the employee was able to claim against the new employer for an injury caused by the negligence of the original employer. The tribunal in the case had said that he could not.

9

Termination of Employment

Continuity, notice and dismissal

***The General of the Salvation Army v Dewsbury* (1984)**
The EDT is that in the contract which may not be the date first worked

***Hill v CA Parsons & Co Ltd* (1972)**
The notice period may depend on the service and status of the employee

***Western Excavating v Sharp* (1978)**
Constructive dismissal must involve a significant breach by the employer going to the root of the contract

Wrongful dismissal

***Eastwood v Magnox Electric plc; McCabe v Cornwall CC* (2004)**
Wrongful dismissal is a claim for breach of contract quite separate to unfair dismissal rights

***Laws v London Chronicle* (1959)**
May include where the breach leading to the dismissal is not sufficiently serious

Termination of employment

Unfair dismissal

***Davison v Kent Meters Ltd* (1975)**
An employee cannot be dismissed for lack of capability if they have not been trained how to do the job

***Taylor v Alidair Ltd* (1978)**
Even summary dismissal for a single act can be justified if the misconduct is sufficiently serious

***St John of God (Care Services) Ltd v Brook* (1992)**
A dismissal to avoid financial difficulty and inconsistency in working practices can be justified as fair

***Iceland Frozen Foods Ltd v Jones* (1983)**
Dismissal is fair if it falls within a reasonable range of responses

***John Lewis plc v Coyne* (2001)**
A dismissal that does not follow proper procedure e.g. proper investigation may be unfair

Redundancy

***Williams v Compare Maxim Ltd* (1982)**
Selection for redundancy must be made according to fair criteria

***Johnson v Nottinghamshire Combined Police Authority* (1974)**
If there is still a need for the work to be done there is no redundancy

Termination other than by dismissal

***Egg Stores Ltd v Leibovic* (1977)**
A contract can be frustrated for illness where it goes on too long

***Ely v YKK Fasteners* (1993)**
Resignation must be genuine and by the employee

***Birch & Humber v The University of Liverpool* (1985)**
A genuine retirement agreement is not a dismissal

9.1 Continuity, notice and dismissal

R v Secretary of State for Employment ex p Seymour-Smith and Perez (No 2) [2000] IRLR 263

Key Facts

At the time of the case the qualifying period of continuous employment for unfair dismissal was two years. Two women wished to claim unfair dismissal but they lacked the necessary two years' continuous service. In a novel action they argued that they were being discriminated against by the law requiring two years' continuous service. They did so on the basis that they believed that the number of women who could comply with the requirement was significantly lower than the number of men who could, obviously because of career breaks for pregnancy and childcare.

Key Law

The House of Lords (now the Supreme Court) referred the case to the European Court of Justice under the Art 177 (now Art 267) procedure. Included in the questions that the House wished clarification on were whether the issue fell within the scope of Art 119 (now Art 157), and whether on that basis the women were entitled to compensation. The European Court of Justice (ECJ) held that it could indeed fall under Art 119 (now Art 157) TFEU if the qualifying period had a disproportionate effect on women. It also identified:

1. that the alleged discriminatory rule was a legitimate aim of the UK's social policy
2. that this aim was unrelated to any discrimination based on sex
3. that the means chosen were suitable for achieving the aim.

The House of Lords did find that there was a disparity in the order of ten women to nine men but in effect that this was insufficient to represent real discrimination.

Key Comment

It is interesting that, with the ECJ judgment coming nine years after the initial case, a new government had already reduced the qualifying period to one year (the current government plan is to change it back to two years). A more interesting point is that had the case succeeded it would have arguably meant that any qualifying period would have been unlawful.

 (EAT) ## Sweeney v J & S Henderson [1999] IRLR 306

Key Facts

The claimant resigned on Saturday and left to start other employment. He then regretted his decision to leave and started back with his old employer on the following Friday. It was later necessary to determine whether that period was a break in the employee's continuous service.

Key Law

It was held that a break in continuous service does not occur unless there is a complete week in which the employee is not employed. Thus the week counted towards continuous service even though there was a short gap in his employment.

 (EAT) ## The General of the Salvation Army v Dewsbury [1984] IRLR 222

Key Facts

A part-time teacher changed to a full-time contract commencing on 1st May. 3rd May was a bank holiday so she did not actually work on either the first or third days of her new contract. She was dismissed with effect from 1st May in the following year and the question was whether she had one year's continuous service.

Key Law

The court held that the date of commencement is that which is stated in the contract and that this may not be the date on which the employee actually first works.

 (IT) ## Futty v D & D Brekkes Ltd [1974] IRLR 130

Key Facts

Dock workers commonly used abusive language in their everyday banter. Futty was a fish filleter and on one occasion his supervisor used a four-letter word and in effect told him where to go. Futty left and found himself another job and then claimed unfair dismissal.

Key Law

The tribunal accepted that abusive language was a common feature of the workplace where Futty worked used by everyone. On this basis he had resigned rather than be dismissed. He could not complain that the abusive language was a significantly serious breach of contract in the circumstances to amount to a dismissal.

(CA) Western Excavating v Sharp [1978] QB 761

Key Facts

Sharp was suspended from work without pay during disciplinary proceedings. He was short of money so he asked for an advance on wages that would be due on his return to work. His employer refused and so Sharp resigned and claimed constructive dismissal.

Key Law

It was held that the refusal was not so serious as to amount to a breach of contract and certainly not a serious breach of contract. His unfair dismissal claim failed.

Key Judgment

Lord Denning explained the test for determining whether a constructive dismissal amounts to a breach: *'If the employer is guilty of conduct which is a significant breach going to the root of the contract of employment or which shows that the employer no longer intends to be bound by one or more of the essential terms of the contract; then the employee is entitled to treat himself as discharged from any further performance. If he does so, then he terminates the contract by reason of the employer's conduct. He is constructively dismissed.'*

(EAT) Alcan Extrusions v Yates [1996] IRLR 327

Key Facts

The employer had unilaterally made quite dramatic changes to the working conditions including working hours, changed shifts and weekend and bank holiday working, and to shift payment. Employees worked under the changed conditions under protest, and arguing that they retained their rights to redundancy and unfair dismissal claims. Eventually some did claim unfair dismissal.

Key Law

Both the tribunal and the EAT agreed that there was a dismissal, an essential feature of unfair dismissal claims. The EAT rejected the employer's argument that unilateral variations of the contract are only a potentially repudiatory breach giving the employee the right only to resign and claim constructive dismissal. It held that significant changes to the original contract made unilaterally can amount to a breach of contract in their own right.

(CA) Hill v CA Parsons & Co Ltd [1972] Ch 305

Key Facts

An employer had reached a 'closed shop' agreement with a trade union. This is an agreement where all employees have to belong to the union. The employer then wrote to the claimant, who refused to join the union, giving him one month's notice of his dismissal. The claimant was a senior engineer with 35 years' service and sought an injunction to lengthen the period of notice.

Key Law

The court allowed the injunction and extended the notice period to six months which it felt was a reasonable period. The employer in fact had no problem with the claimant but was acting under pressure from the trade union.

Key Comment

In fact the court was eager to grant the injunction because by the end of the renewed notice period the Industrial Relations Act would be in force and this would make the closed shop agreement unlawful and mean that any dismissal of the claimant was unfair.

9.2 Wrongful dismissal

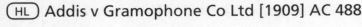

(HL) Addis v Gramophone Co Ltd [1909] AC 488

Key Facts

A manager was dismissed from his post and his employer had replaced him with a new manager even before he left. He claimed for wrongful dismissal and also sought damages for the humiliation and distress caused by the manner of his exit from the business.

Key Law

While acknowledging his wrongful dismissal, the House of Lords refused his claim for damages for injury to his reputation caused by the improper dismissal and also for the mental distress caused by the humiliating manner of his dismissal. The proper place for this according to Lord Atkin rather than a contractual claim would have been under the tort of defamation. The court held that he could recover only for the loss of salary and commission owed.

(HL) Johnson v Unisys Ltd [2001] IRLR 279

Key Facts

The claimant was a director who had been employed by the company for twenty years and over a period of time suffered stress. He was summarily dismissed in breach of the company's disciplinary procedure following some vague allegations of misconduct and developed a severe psychiatric illness as a result. He claimed unfair dismissal and a breach of the implied term of mutual trust and confidence. The issue was whether he should be awarded in excess of the then limit for unfair dismissal claims of £11,000 since the claimant was arguing that the unfair manner of his dismissal had caused him financial loss.

Key Law

The House of Lords (now the Supreme Court) accepted his claim for unfair dismissal but held that to create a parallel right to damages in excess of the limit would be to go against Parliament's clear intentions.

(HL) Eastwood v Magnox Electric plc; McCabe v Cornwall CC [2004] IRLR 733

Key Facts

In joint appeals both appellants had been dismissed following lengthy but flawed disciplinary procedures. Eastwood had successfully claimed unfair dismissal resulting from a grudge against him by his manager, the procedure leading up to dismissal taking ten months. McCabe was a teacher who had been accused of improper behaviour with young female pupils where the disciplinary process leading to dismissal took more than two years. Both also claimed damages for breach of contract and negligence.

Key Law

Eastwood's appeal succeeded and McCabe's was dismissed.
The House of Lords held that the cause of action in common law
accrued before any dismissals occurred and suggested that *Johnson
v Unisys* should be reconsidered.

(CA) Laws v London Chronicle [1959] 1 WLR 698

Key Facts

Laws was employed as an assistant to an advertising manager for a
newspaper. After only working for the newspaper for three weeks
she was summarily dismissed. She attended an editorial meeting
with her manager and had followed him when he walked out,
despite being ordered to stay by the managing director. She was
dismissed without notice for her act of disobedience and argued
that this was a wrongful dismissal.

Key Law

The court held that her actions were neither wilful nor
sufficiently serious to amount to a breach of a fundamental term
of her contract to obey lawful and reasonable orders. As a result
she had been wrongfully dismissed and was entitled to claim for
damages.

9.3 Unfair dismissal

(IT) Davison v Kent Meters Ltd [1975] IRLR 145

Key Facts

An assembly worker was dismissed for lack of capability for
wrongly assembling 500 components. She argued that she
had followed the process shown her by her supervisor but he
claimed that he had in fact never shown her how to assemble the
components.

Key Law

The court held that the dismissal was unfair. The evidence of the
supervisor indicated that she had never been properly instructed
in assembling the components and she could not be held to be
incapable without adequate instruction.

(EAT) Bevan Harris Ltd v Gair [1981] IRLR 520

 Key Facts

A foreman who had given eleven years' service was eventually dismissed after consistently poor performance and four warnings. He claimed unfair dismissal.

Key Law

The tribunal initially upheld his claim on the basis that the employer should have considered reasonable alternatives before dismissing him and here the employee could have been demoted. However, the EAT overturned this on appeal. The employer had considered demotion but decided against it because it was a small business and there was a loss of confidence in the employee. As such the dismissal fell within the 'reasonable range of responses' test.

(IT) Coulson v Felixstowe Dock & Railway Co Ltd [1975] IRLR 11

 Key Facts

The employee suffered sickness absences over a long period and was eventually put on lighter work. He was also informed that he would be given six months in which to show that he was fit. When he suffered further illness and sickness absence he was dismissed and claimed unfair dismissal.

 Key Law

It was held that the dismissal was fair since the employer had made reasonable steps to allow the employee to continue and to accommodate his illnesses. However, there has to come a time when, in fairness to the employer and the necessities of the business, that a constantly ill employee can be dismissed.

(EAT) Converform (Darwen) Ltd v Bell [1981] IRLR 195

 Key Facts

A director suffered from a heart attack and had time off work. When he had recovered his employer refused to let him back to work arguing that he was at risk of another heart attack. The director claimed unfair dismissal.

Key Law

It was held that the risk of another heart attack alone could not be a fair ground for dismissal under capability. It would only be relevant if the risk made it unsafe for the employee in his work.

(CA) Taylor v Alidair Ltd [1978] IRLR 82

Key Facts

A pilot through his incompetence landed a plane very badly causing a great deal of damage. He was subsequently dismissed on capability and claimed unfair dismissal.

Key Law

It was held that even a small departure from expected high standards might justify dismissal in certain cases because of the potential consequences of not dismissing.

(CA) Dietman v London Borough of Brent [1988] IRLR 146

Key Facts

A clause in a contract defined gross misconduct for which summary dismissal was available. After an inquiry the employee was found to be grossly negligent in her duties.

Key Law

The court held that gross negligence did not fall under the employer's contractual definition of gross misconduct so the employee was unfairly dismissed.

(IT) Mathieson v W J Noble [1972] IRLR 76

Key Facts

A salesman, who was required to drive, was then disqualified from driving. He made his own arrangements to be able to continue his work, hiring a chauffeur to drive him and was happy to stand the cost. His employer however did not accept this and dismissed him.

Key Law

Ordinarily where something like a clean driving licence is a requirement of employment a dismissal in circumstances such as these would be fair. Here however the dismissal was accepted as unfair since the employer had not acted reasonably in failing to see whether the arrangement proved satisfactory.

(EAT) St John of God (Care Services) Ltd v Brook [1992] IRLR 546

Key Facts

A charity-run hospital where NHS funding had been reduced faced possible closure. The employer proposed to cut pay and benefits to the staff to make the necessary savings to avoid going out of business. The changes were accepted by 140 of the 170 employees and four of those refusing were eventually dismissed.

Key Law

The dismissals were held to be fair for any other substantial reason, an economic, technical or organisational reason. This was because the other employees had accepted the changes and the firm ran the risk of collapse without the changes.

(HL) Council of Civil Service Unions v Minister for the Civil Service [1985] ICR 14

Key Facts

The government had decided that staff at an intelligence base, GCHQ, should be prevented from being members of a trade union because of a potential risk to security. Some members held out and were dismissed and challenged the decision.

Key Law

On the issue of judicial review it was held that the government could only be challenged on the way that it made its decision, not on the merits of the decision. The decision and the dismissals were for a substantial reason.

(EAT) British Home Stores Ltd v Burchell [1980] ICR 303

Key Facts

Burchell was dismissed as part of group who had allegedly made dishonest staff purchases. The company began an investigation and Burchell was implicated by a colleague. Burchell argued that the employer had not proved her dishonesty and that therefore her dismissal was unfair.

Key Law

It was held that it was sufficient that the employer had a reasonable belief and had investigated the allegations. The EAT also identified the basic test (known as the 'reasonable range of responses' test):

- there must be a genuine belief in the grounds for the dismissal
- this must be based on reasonable grounds
- there must have been a reasonable investigation, and
- there must have been reasonable grounds to dismiss found.

Iceland Frozen Foods Ltd v Jones [1983] ICR 17

Key Facts

Jones was a shift foreman on a night shift. He was dismissed when he forgot to lock up the premises at the end of the shift. He then claimed unfair dismissal when he was dismissed.

Key Law

The tribunal failed to apply the test in s 98(4) Employment Rights Act 1996 so the EAT held that the dismissal was unfair. However, it developed the five-stage test for determining fairness (the reasonable range of responses test from *British Homes Stores v Burchell*):

(i)   The test starts with s 98(4) ERA 1996 – determination of whether dismissal fair or unfair (having regards to reasons given by employer) a) depends on whether in the circumstances (including size and administrative resources of the business) the employer acted reasonably in treating it as sufficient grounds for dismissal, and b) this is determined in accordance with equity and the substantial merits of the case

(ii) the tribunal must consider whether the employer acted reasonably – not whether or not they think the dismissal was fair

(iii) the tribunal must not substitute its own decision as to what the right course was for the employer to adopt

(iv) there is a band of reasonable responses to the employee's conduct in which different employers might take different views

(v)   the function of the tribunal is to determine whether the dismissal fell within the reasonable range of responses that a reasonable employer might take.

Key Link

Haddon v Van den Bergh's Foods Ltd [1999] IRLR 672 where the Court of Appeal suggested that there is nothing intrinsically wrong in the tribunal substituting its own view for that of the employer (this in effect is to ignore the 'range of reasonable responses' test) – but in *Midland Bank v Madden* [2000] IRLR 827 the EAT suggested that no court short of the Court of Appeal can discard the range of reasonable responses test, although accepting that the *Burchill* test might simply go to the reason for the dismissal rather than its reasonableness.

(HL) Polkey v AE Dayton Services Ltd [1988] AC 344

Key Facts

Polkey was made redundant after a reorganisation within the company. He was not consulted but he was called into the manager's office and dismissed and sent home. He claimed unfair dismissal arguing that the code of practice in operation at the time had not been followed.

Key Law

The tribunal upheld the dismissal as fair on the basis that the failure to consult would not have made any difference to his selection for redundancy. The House of Lords (now the Supreme Court) held that the dismissal was unfair since there was no way of ascertaining what the result would have been if the employer had adopted the correct procedure.

Key Judgment

Lord Bridge identified that: *'An employer having* prima facie *grounds to dismiss for [a potentially fair reason] will in the great majority of cases not act reasonably in treating the reason as a sufficient reason for dismissal unless and until he has taken the steps, conveniently classified in most of the authorities as "procedural", which are necessary in the circumstances of the case to justify the action.'*

CA Hollister v National Farmers' Union [1979] IRLR 238

Key Facts

The National Farmers Union (NFU) operates an insurance business and was in the process of reorganising it which involved changes to the contracts of employment of the staff. One insurance salesman would not accept the changes to his contract and was dismissed as a result and claimed unfair dismissal. The NFU argued that the dismissal was fair because the changes to the contract were necessary for the improvements in the running of the business.

Key Law

It was held that the changes to the contracts were essential to the business and represented a sufficiently substantial reason for the dismissal which was fair.

EAT John Lewis plc v Coyne [2001] IRLR 139

Key Facts

Coyne was employed by John Lewis for nearly 14 years and had an exemplary work record. She was dismissed when it was found that she had made 111 personal telephone calls on the work's telephone in work's time contrary to the disciplinary code. She was dismissed without any meaningful investigation.

Key Law

Because of the absence of a proper disciplinary investigation the dismissal did not follow the procedural requirements in the ACAS Code. It was an unfair dismissal despite being for a potentially fair reason for dismissal – conduct.

9.4 Redundancy

EAT Williams v Compare Maxim Ltd [1982] ICR 156

Key Facts

The company was in financial difficulties and decided on a redundancy scheme in order to survive. It told the trade union representatives that there would be redundancies, but no actual consultation with either the union or the staff occurred on either the criteria to be used or the identity of staff at risk. Williams was one of the staff who was dismissed without any warning.

Key Law

The EAT laid down guidelines on the correct approach and held the dismissal unfair on the basis that it offended all commonly accepted standards of fairness.

Key Judgment

Browne-Wilkinson J stated: *'The basic approach is that, in the unfortunate circumstances that necessarily attend redundancies, as much as is reasonably possible should be done to mitigate the impact on the work force and to satisfy them that the selection has been made fairly and not on the basis of personal whim ...'*

(CA) Johnson v Nottinghamshire Combined Police Authority [1974] ICR 170

Key Facts

Two Police Authority clerical workers worked shifts from 9.30 am until 5.30 pm. They were then required to change to a new split-shift system with shifts from 8.00 am. until 3.00 pm, and 1.00 am until 8.00 am. They were dismissed after refusing to work under the new shift system and claimed that instead they had been made redundant because of the significant change in the shift patterns.

Key Law

It was held that there was no redundancy. In redundancy it is the job not the employee that is made redundant. In this case the Authority still needed two clerical workers, merely at different times.

(HL) Murray v Foyle Meats Ltd [1999] ICR 827

Key Facts

Two men were employed in an abattoir as 'meat plant operatives'. There were two halls and a loading bay but the men always worked in one hall. Their line was closed down and the men tried to rely on a flexibility clause in their contract. This required them to do any job in the abattoir, so they argued that their dismissal was not therefore a redundancy and that it was unfair selection since they could have merely been moved elsewhere in the abattoir.

Key Law

The issue clearly concerned redundancy based on diminution of the need for the work. The House of Lords (now the Supreme Court) explained that the key issue for tribunals to consider is whether or not the dismissal is attributable to a diminution. If so then there is no need to consider what is in the contract.

(QBD) Taylor v Kent CC [1969] 2 QB 560

Key Facts

A headmaster of a school was made redundant and offered alternative work as a supply teacher, although his salary and other benefits were to remain the same. He rejected the offer of alternative work and argued for a redundancy payment. The school in turn argued that his unreasonable refusal to accept the work meant that he was ineligible for a redundancy payment.

Key Law

The court accepted the argument that the offer of work was not a suitable alternative since it meant a significant reduction in status. As such he was entitled to a redundancy payment.

(EAT) Rank Xerox Ltd v Churchill [1988] IRLR 280

Key Facts

Churchill worked for Rank Xerox in its London headquarters. Her contract included a mobility clause in the following terms: 'The company may require you to transfer to another location.' The company did then move its headquarters out of London. Churchill refused to move and claimed that, since her place of work no longer existed, she was entitled to a redundancy payment.

Key Law

The EAT held that, for the purposes of redundancy, place of work means place of work as required by the contract rather than the actual place of work where the employee has worked. As a result her place of work had only moved and not ceased to exist and she was not redundant.

O'Brien v Associated Fire Alarms Ltd [1968] 1 WLR 1916

 Key Facts

O'Brien and a number of colleagues worked for the company in the Liverpool area. When there was a shortage of work they were told that they had to work in Barrow, a distance of 150 miles from Liverpool, although there was no mobility clause in their contract. Since this made it impossible for them to see their families except at weekends they resigned and argued that they were redundant. The employer asked the court to imply a mobility clause into the contracts.

 Key Law

It was held that no such clause could be implied. Since the men had worked around the Liverpool area for many years and there had never formerly been any question of the men relocating they were indeed redundant and entitled to a redundancy payment.

Bass Leisure Ltd v Thomas [1994] IRLR 104

 Key Facts

Thomas worked at a depot in Coventry and her contract included a mobility clause. Her employers then asked her to transfer to a depot twenty miles away. She refused and claimed that she had in effect been made redundant.

 Key Law

The EAT agreed. It held that the true test should be a geographical test rather than a contractual one. On this basis the additional daily travel meant that operation of the clause was unreasonable and she was indeed redundant and entitled to a redundancy payment.

Commission for Healthcare Audit & Inspection v Ward [2008] UKEAT 0579 07

Key Facts

Following a restructure of the organisation for which she worked the claimant's job had ceased to exist. She was offered alternative employment on three occasions and indeed asked for further information on the post on several occasions but rejected the post claiming that it was not a suitable alternative. She argued instead that she was entitled to a redundancy payment.

Key Law

The EAT agreed with the findings of the tribunal that, while there was no reduction in status, there were a number of material differences between the two posts and, although it was marginally suitable, it was not an ideal replacement for her old job so that it was reasonable for her to reject it.

Key Judgment

It was stated that: *'In an appropriate case where the offer of alternative work is overwhelmingly suitable it may be easier for the employer to show that a refusal by the employee is unreasonable. It is part of the balancing act which the tribunal is charged to carry out.'*

9.5 Termination other than by dismissal

(EAT) Egg Stores Ltd v Leibovici [1977] ICR 260

Key Facts

An employee was absent from work for four months after an accident. The employer continued to pay his wages until January 1975. In April 1975 the employee asked if he could now return to work but he was refused as the employer had now got someone else doing his job. The issue was whether or not the contract was frustrated.

Key Law

The court offered guidelines for where frustration does occur: even though at the time of the event the outcome was uncertain; the time has come where the situation has gone on for so long and the prospects of return so low that it is no longer practical for the contract to continue.

Key Comment

The court also recognised that the following should be taken into account: the length of employment with the employer; the expected length e.g. indefinitely or length of fixed term; the nature of the work; the nature, length and effect of the illness; the employer's need to appoint a replacement; the risk to the employer of incurring further risk of e.g. obligation to pay redundancy or unfair dismissal; whether the employer has continued to pay the employee; acts and comments of the employer e.g. the manner of dismissal; the likely reaction of a reasonable employer in the circumstances; the prospect of the employee recovering.

➤ Key Links

Paal Wilson & Co v Partenreederei Hannah Blumenthal [1983] 1 AC 854 HL where it was identified that there must be a) some unforeseen change in the outside circumstances and not provided for by the parties which prevents performance; and b) the event was not the fault of either party.

(CA) Ely v YKK Fasteners [1993] IRLR 500

Key Facts

An employee informed his employer that he was contemplating emigrating to Australia and had applied for work there. The employee later changed his mind and informed the employer about this but by that stage the employer had found a replacement for him and considered the contract at an end. The issue for the court was whether there was voluntary resignation or whether the termination of the contract was a dismissal.

Key Law

The court held that, because the employer had only informed his employer of his plans and not yet resigned, it was a dismissal. However, in the circumstances it was held to be a fair dismissal for other substantial reason.

(CA) Birch & Humber v The University of Liverpool [1985] IRLR 165

Key Facts

The university sent out a circular to its lecturing staff asking for volunteers for early retirement who would be given enhanced retirement payments. Two lecturers volunteered for the scheme and agreed to their leaving dates. However, after leaving they then argued that they had been dismissed and were entitled to redundancy payments.

Key Law
Their claim failed because there had to be a genuine agreement in order for the early retirement to take place and the lecturers to gain their enhanced payment. The termination was by mutual agreement and was not a dismissal.

Igbo v Johnson Matthey Chemicals Ltd
CA [1986] IRLR 215

Key Facts
A signed contract of employment included a clause specifying that failure to return on a due date after extended leave automatically terminated the contract. The employee failed to return on the due date but was actually ill at the time.

Key Law
It was held that there was no mutual agreement to terminate the contract. As a result the termination was a dismissal. Otherwise it would have conflicted with the employee's statutory rights.

Index